Copyright © 2015-8
By Alex Echols, Andrew Gottlieb,
and Sulinya Ramanan

Cover Design: Marko Polic

All Rights Reserved. No part of this text or the images herein may be reproduced, transmitted, decompiled, reverse engineered, or distributed without the express written permission of the authors – other than for "fair use" as brief quotations embodied in articles and reviews.

The authors of this book do not dispense medical advice or prescribe the use of any technique as a form of treatment for physical, emotional, or medical problems without the advice of a physician, either directly or indirectly. The intent of the authors is only to offer information of a general nature to help you on your journey. In the event you use any of the information in this book for yourself, the authors and the publisher assume no responsibility for your actions.

This book and project is dedicated to our family, friends, and all the dreamers throughout the world.

2nd Edition

Foreword

"The Two-Week Notice is your guide to unapologetically stepping into your greatness in your business and life."

-Lisa Nichols, *New York Times* Bestselling Author and International Speaker

Table of Contents

Introduction _____ 1
   Chapter 1: Awakening the Dreamer _____ 5
Section I _____ 14
Finding the Entrepreneur _____ 14
   Chapter 2: How to Discover Your Passions _____ 15
   Chapter 3: The Shift _____ 30
   Chapter 4: How to Quit _____ 44
   Chapter 5: Transitioning Out _____ 58
Section II _____ 67
Nurturing the Entrepreneur _____ 67
   Chapter 6: Changing Tracks _____ 68
   Chapter 7: Entrepreneurial Depression _____ 73
   Chapter 8: Mindset, Self-Trust and Emotional Health _____ 79
   Chapter 9: Good Physical Health _____ 94
Section III _____ 102
Connecting the Entrepreneur _____ 102
   Chapter 10: Connecting More Authentically _____ 103

Chapter 11: Outgrowing and Elevating Your Network _____ 111

Chapter 12: Finding a Mentor _____ 115

Section IV _____ 121

Growing the Entrepreneur _____ 121

Chapter 13: Building Collaborations and Partnerships _____ 122

Chapter 14: Build Your Brand _____ 132

Chapter 15: Find Your Tribe _____ 135

Chapter 16: Finding Joy in the Entrepreneurial Journey_____ 142

Chapter 17: The Journey Continues _____ 148

Section V _____ 150

Bonus Chapters _____ 150

Chapter 18: Women in Entrepreneurship _____ 151

Chapter 19: Savings Accounts and Good Health _____ 155

Chapter 20: Creating a For-Benefit Organization _____ 159

About the Authors_____ 168

Introduction

Why We Wrote This Book

Did you know that only 13% of all people worldwide enjoy going to work (McGregor)? If you are one among the overwhelming majority of people who do not, you are projected to spend an average of 90,000 hours of your life doing work that you dislike (Shontell). If you are reading this book, you clearly value your time, missions, impact, and freedom too much to allow these statistics to become your fate.

Nonetheless, you have probably been handed a standard model of work that just does not fit your definition of a passionate, fulfilling life. You might have had jobs in which you have felt trapped and unhappy, or you might be working such a job right now. Perhaps you are even one among the two-thirds of young workers who, on the first day of their new jobs, have already started to think about alternative employment (Carroll). Irrespective of your situation, you are reading this because the standard work model has failed you. And, in fact, that model has been failing for a long time.

Let us first look at the financial return on investment of education in the current job market. At the time of this book's writing, Millennials have amassed $1 Trillion in student loan debt (Louis). That is more than five percent of the United States Gross Domestic Product (World Bank). On average, Americans in their twenties have

$45,000 worth of debt, the majority of which comes from student loans (Berman).

As a result, Millennials are on track to become the most educated generation in American history and yet have an unemployment rate that is nearly twice the national average (Picci). And of those who are employed, sixty percent of Millennials feel they do not make enough money (Pew Research), and rightfully so. Very often, salaries do not keep up with inflation, and half of all human resource departments have not adjusted recruiting salaries in the past 3 to 5 years (Schawbel).

If you are female or a minority, your return on investment is projected to be even worse. Wage inequality remains an enormous problem. In 2012, women made only 77.5 cents for every dollar that men earned while working the same jobs (Graves). Women still represent less than five percent of CEOs at major American companies (Fairchild). Racial and ethnic disparities are even more striking. In 2013, the median net worth of the average white household was ten times as large as that of the average Hispanic household and thirteen times as great as the average black household (Fry).

There are other problems, too. Our jobs take a serious toll on our health and wellness. Nearly half of Americans report that they have gained weight at their current job. Forty percent of employees state that their jobs are very or extremely stressful, and the illnesses that result from stress cost companies more than 13 Million working days (Shontell). Negative job environments also lead to vastly

Introduction

higher divorce rates and unhappy parents are strongly correlated with children who become bullies in school (Dinsmore).

Do you want to leave your emotional, physical, and financial well-being in the hands of the job market described above, or do you want to reclaim your power and create the life you desire? Do you want to move through life as a corporate marionette or do you want to direct what you create? Do you want to allow social corruption to stay as it is, or do you want to uplift society and leave a lasting mark on the world? If you picked the latter choice to either of these questions, you are in very good company.

We are the generation of change-makers. For the first time, sixty-one percent of the emerging generation of workers feels personally responsible to make a difference (Nelson), and eighty-four percent state that doing so is even more important than professional recognition. Ninety-two percent believe that business success should be measured by metrics other than just financial profit (Schawbel). We are unlike any generation in history.

Lastly, like sixty-nine percent of young people, you very likely want more freedom at work (Rasmussen College). You want your efforts to be measured not by hours at a location, but by the output of what you do. Sixty percent of Millennials desire location freedom and schedule flexibility. In fact, a study by PwC reports that many Millennials would give up pay or delay a promotion to achieve an ideal schedule. And a third of young professionals prioritize social media freedom over salary in accepting a job offer

(PwC). Unfortunately, if you desire any of these features, only a small section of the job market will afford you these benefits. Overall, the economy is slow to restructure itself to changing demands.

The good news is that taking control of your dreams is more doable than ever before. Nearly half of Generation Y wants to start a business in the next five years, and over one-third of employed Millennials have already started businesses on the side to supplement their incomes (Schawbel). If you have big dreams, you do not have to wait to bring them to life.

The goal of this book is to show you how to do that and to tell you what being an entrepreneur feels like. This book is not written from the perspective of someone who made it years ago and is giving you an account that has become rosier with age. Instead, we are people just like you who are providing you with a raw and immersive journey of three young entrepreneurs with all their joys, trials, and uncertainties. We show you the lessons that we have learned through real experience. We are here to inspire and empower you to take the passion in your soul and turn it into something extraordinary.

You define the new economy. Let's go!

Chapter 1:

Awakening the Dreamer

"All our dreams can come true if we have the courage to pursue them." –Walt Disney

It truly feels like just a few days ago.

Imagine a chubby little boy being sent home with a bad behavior notice for sitting in class and daydreaming, mumbling to himself, and joking with others. One would envision that such a kid would be quite the class clown and chaos maker.

But there was something different, maybe even a bit odd, about this young boy. He did not intend to be a rabble-rouser – he was just a youngin' who had not learned how to contain his curiosity and happiness within the school setting.

The Two-Week Notice

Now imagine how the young boy's big chestnut eyes expanded as he imagined new ideas with wonder and excitement. He was full of dreams. Naturally, he wanted to share them with others.

Now, visualize him growing into a young man with that same wonder and soon figuring out that his daydreams could become his reality if he wanted them enough.

Does this story remind you of yourself or someone you know? For me, this story is very personal: I was that little boy.

It does not feel that long ago when I was sitting in my fourth grade Junior Achievement (JA) class, listening to guest speakers while daydreaming. JA was a program that taught fundamentals of entrepreneurship, financial literacy, and strategy to younger children.

Starting early, right? In our workbooks, we had to complete various exercises in addition to writing down some of our biggest aspirations and life goals. One page asked, "If you could pick a career or a person to be like when you grow up, what or who would you choose?"

I knew my answer immediately: Walt Disney.

Luckily, I had given this question much thought before. From a very young age, I was inspired not only by Disney's classics and my all-time favorite, The Lion King, but also by the culture that Disney created in his company. I imagined that when I grew up, I would be just like him, bringing happiness and joy to millions of people through movies, theme parks and other attractions throughout the world.

And from there, my dream to one day be able to give back in major ways began to flourish. Walt Disney's inspiration and genius have nurtured the seed of entrepreneurship within me ever since. And as I grew older, my environment gave me more momentum. Let me explain.

Growing up on the South Side of Chicago, it was not cool to want to be a businessperson. Being young, black and successful meant being a rapper, basketball player or hustler, nothing else. Many of my peers bought into this definition of success and became trapped by it. I was not exceptional in sports, and I sucked at rapping. So given the popular framework, my options seemed limited. Fortunately, I had an incredible support system of family members and friends who urged me to know my worth, find my strengths and passions (even if they were not basketball or rap), and cultivate them.

At the age of 13, I unofficially became an entrepreneur by starting my own graphic design business. Back then, I did not have the leisure of setting up ads and connecting with potential leads through Facebook, Twitter and the rest of the Internet. Instead, I worked directly with many of the members of my father's church and the parents of the students who attended my elementary school. From brochures to logos to flyers, I was your go to man (or boy) when you needed something done for cheaper than the market rate.

The Two-Week Notice

In high school and college, this passion for entrepreneurship led me to join several leadership organizations and take on leading roles in my Latin and Hindu dance groups. Then I discovered a new passion that lit my dreams on fire: international travel. At seventeen, I took my first trip outside the US, and I was hooked on to learning more about different cultures, practices, foods and mindsets.

In his bestselling memoir Honeymoon with my Brother, Franz Wisner notes, "travel is the only investment you can make that has a guaranteed return." I have found this to be universally true.

With deep gratitude to Walt Disney, my amazing family and support system, and that first trip abroad that completely reframed my views of the world and of life itself, my inner dreamer had been awakened. I was hungry for more of life's adventures, and for the chance to bring happiness, peace and joy to millions of people throughout the world.

But first, I had to keep discovering what that meant to me.

Awakening the Dreamer

People recognize the need to step into their greatness at different stages of life. The bullying I experienced as a kid robbed me of my confidence and the constant voices of others emphasized my faults instead of my positive attributes. Unbeknownst to me, these emotional scars stayed with me for years until I became aware of the perception I had created about myself. Without my knowledge, I had been projecting my negative beliefs about myself into the world. Other people responded by treating me accordingly, perpetuating my cycle of unhappiness.

When I recognized my lack of self-love, I realized that I needed to make drastic changes and discard my negative opinions. I believe that the best way to gain confidence is by putting yourself completely outside of your comfort zone. So instead of returning to my hometown after my sophomore year of college, I interned in a new city.

While searching for internships after my sophomore year, I stumbled across something called Dream Careers. It is a global internship company that packages together a total acclimation process for a summer internship. Not only did it promise a dream internship in my dream city, but it also came with housing, meal plans, weekend activities, and seminars. Dream Careers had over 200 other college students in the program. It came across to me as a mixture of Disneyland, TED Talks and the possibility of interning on Wall Street, which I deemed as my goal because it was what all the smart people did. As a super Type A personality in college, I wanted a prestigious career that would make me a lot of money. I was not concerned about anything else but the size of my bank account and the status symbol my job gave me.

That summer, the dreamer within me awakened. Before the experience with Dream Careers, I was merely sleeping as I walked through life. I had no sense of purpose or direction and was guided by what others thought was best for me.

However, by the end of the summer, a new Andrew had emerged because I was living in a completely new city, meeting friends from all over the world, and discovering what I wanted to do with my life. By stepping outside of my comfort to such an extreme level, I had found my inner voice that had been waiting to emerge my entire life.

I was confident enough to go after the things I wanted and listen to my intuition. All it took were some amazing friends and experiences to show me that life is simply what you make of it. If you do not believe you are worthy or capable, then your beliefs will become a self-fulfilling prophecy. On the other hand, if you believe in possibility and are optimistic, life can be a beautiful journey.

After feeling this renewed sense of purpose that summer, I started to think about my purpose in life. How could I make an impact in the world instead of viewing life as a contest to see how much money I could make? I knew that helping other people would be a central theme for the rest of my life because of the support I received that summer. My new friends, business contacts and bosses helped me to see my full potential that was waiting to be brought to the surface. And if I could spend the rest of my life helping people in the same manner, then that was what I wanted to create as my life's work.

While I did not realize it then, I had just embarked upon my personal legend.

I hope that by reading through our insights on following your heart, you will understand that the unlimited potential and happiness you seek does not rest on some unattainable mountain. In reality, it is, and always has been, inside you.

I handed over my laptop, ran outside, and started dancing with joy. Whoever was monitoring the parking lot surveillance cameras that day must have had a good laugh. But thankfully, everyone else within a one-mile radius of me was neatly tucked away in a cubicle. I had been waiting for this moment for so long, when I could finally leave my job and run my own show. I promised myself that I would never again live my life on anyone else's terms. Finally, I had everything figured out and was eager to share what I believed was expert knowledge.

Needless to say, it was not that easy.

Now, months later, I have scrapped what I wrote twice, and I will tell you that you can never have a true understanding of what entrepreneurship entails until you have immersed yourself in it. All too often, literature on entrepreneurship comes from the perspective of someone who made it years ago, and is devoid of details concerning how and why starting a business is so challenging. Our main goal in this book is to provide you with an honest perspective of being immersed in the journey, with all its wonders and pitfalls, and serve as a guide for you when you need some help navigating your own.

In the year prior to leaving my job, I read extensively about entrepreneurship. Many articles talked about how important it is to "step outside of one's comfort zone." That sweet, benign expression always left me feeling warm and fuzzy as I theorized about stepping out of my comfort zone.

One year later, I discovered that it actually translated to something like jumping off a fifty-foot ledge into an ice-cold ocean of uncertainty where I must teach myself to swim in the eight seconds before I go under-because the greatest treasure in the world is waiting on shore, if I can only reach it. Okay, maybe not that dramatic, but it is scary, thrilling, and immensely rewarding.

Awakening the Dreamer

So why go through all this trouble when I could just as easily pursue a cushy corporate job and let someone else pay my way through life? Quite simply, I do not believe I had a choice. I needed to be able to contribute at the highest level possible. I realized very quickly that the level of freedom to create and serve that I desired was not available through corporate work.

My time as a corporate employee was somewhat of a pressure cooker. I was depressed and stuck. But that forced me to dig deep into what I really wanted and cared about. At MIT, I had discovered the healing power of raw food and knew that eventually I wanted pursue a business in wellness. But my dream seemed so far away, and I could not see how to pursue it. Eventually I knew I had to make the leap to entrepreneurship, no matter how impossible it seemed, or lose my dream forever. So I stepped to the edge of that icy cliff, took a deep breath, and jumped.

Our hope is that you are not only inspired to make the same jump yourself, but that you have the tools and knowledge you need to successfully take the leap. This book will help you find what you need.

We invite you to experience this informative, authentic and vulnerable account of three young entrepreneurs who, as you read this, are working to leave the world a better place.

Welcome to The Two-Week Notice.

Section I

Finding the Entrepreneur

Chapter 2: How to Discover Your Passions

"What business do I start? I do not even know what my purpose is!"

"I have way too many ideas and like so many things. How do I pick just one? I am so confused about which way I should go first, or what business I should start."

Have you ever found yourself contemplating one of the questions above? In this chapter, we address both of these. If you already know what business you want to start, great! If not, we are here to help you fix that.

Please note that this is a dense chapter with a lot of work. You do not need to complete all of these assignments in one pass. Rather, we suggest reading through this chapter and coming back to it when you are ready to work through the assignments.

The Two Pillars

As an entrepreneur, there are two basic elements necessary for your success: practicality and passion. Sometimes they can come into conflict, so you will need to balance them.

For your business idea to be viable, you must have an audience or a market that is willing to pay for your products or services. Without a solid strategy, you will not generate revenue. Your team must also be capable of executing on the necessary aspects of bringing your vision to life. In this chapter, we will cover how to discover more about you as well as how to determine whether your business idea is viable or not.

But for your business idea to be possible, you must be *willing* to execute on your objectives, even when you are stressed, dejected, or feel that you are running out of steam. The truth is that as an entrepreneur, you will not have time to sulk or feel sorry for yourself. If you are inherently excited about your idea and you have strong reasons for why you want your business to thrive, the probability of your business succeeding will be much greater. In addition, you might feel compelled, at times, to direct your efforts towards areas of your business that are fun rather than the ones you really should be spending time on. In these times, it is especially critical to be objective and refocus.

If your vision is sufficiently compelling, you will have the capacity to do so.

How to Discover Your Passions

Your business originates from strong motives and is fueled by them. It is brought to life and sustained by consistent, strategic action. Growing a business is exhausting, so if the energy that you receive from running your business does not match up to the energy you expend, your business will not be sustainable.

The Groundwork

How do you determine your passion? Maybe you have struggled to find a business idea behind which you can confidently stand. Perhaps you have read many books on this subject only to finish them and discover that you still do not have an idea. The reality is that thinking alone will not inform you, and no book will actually tell you the answer. Books like this can provide you with invaluable tools and strategies, but you must be willing to take action and experience new situations that can inspire business ideas. Discovering your passion is a fun and active process!

Mindset

First, understand that no idea is ever final. Committing to a business now does not preclude you from starting a different business later. Your first idea does not have to become a blockbuster company that becomes the highlight of your career. It also does not mean that the scope of your business is set in stone. Your business will evolve (as will you!), so allow yourself to be playful and curious as you generate ideas and as you begin the process of building your business. See the process as iterative; your failures are precious data points without which you cannot improve your business or strategies.

Identifying Problems

Every business idea starts by identifying an existing problem, inefficiency, or lack of quality. Even new businesses that are entering highly populated markets must have something new to offer that is desirable. For instance, think about your favorite clothing lines or stores. There are many clothing companies and retailers. What makes your favorite brands different? In particular, what qualities do they bring to the market that would be largely absent without them?

Understand that these factors can be subtle. For instance, in the example of clothing, brands are defined by the feelings they impart. In considering how they design their clothing lines, companies must consider what kind of image their consumers want to portray. They translate these feelings into the pieces they create. For instance, a line that wants to blend novelty with professionalism might feature cuts that are both cleaner and more striking than those of its competition. The most iconic brands are those that are the most distinctive and clear in their values.

In this book, we will take a psychological approach to generating ideas. World-renowned business expert and peak performance coach, Anthony Robbins, teaches that all humans have six fundamental needs:

1. Certainty, Safety, and Security

How to Discover Your Passions

2. Variety, Surprise, and Stimulation
3. Significance
4. Love and Connection
5. Contribution
6. Growth

If you look at your life, you will notice that every problem you have ever faced has been a result of one or more of these needs being unfulfilled or out of balance. The same is true with everyone else. So when it comes to building a business, ask yourself which of these human needs you will be addressing through your products or services. Think about it like this: the more needs you fulfill and the more strongly you meet these needs, the more raving fans you will have!

Ultimately, you are in the business of marketing feelings (even if that feeling is relief from unpleasant feelings). It is important to get very clear on what those feelings are. Given this framework, let's dive into the kinds of problems you want to solve. You have probably done similar exercises, but not as in-depth as what you are about to do. Here, you will identify the core feelings and outcomes you want to create, and then reverse engineer business ideas. First, ask the following basic questions:

1. Are you extremely passionate about anything in particular? If so, the answers should be obvious to you. Now, you might be passionate about something but not want to turn it into a business. For instance, if you are passionate about biking, you might not want to start a company man-

ufacturing bikes or organizing races. That is okay! But let's look a little deeper.

What are the underlying elements of that passion that really excite you, and how do they make you feel? Which of the six human needs listed above does it satisfy? For instance, if you love biking, these underlying elements might include adventure, thrill, exhilaration, movement, nature, the freshness of the air against your face, or sunshine. It could even be the feeling of reconnecting with your most primal nature and feeling one with the Earth and with life. Really get clear on what makes you feel the way you do, and how they make you feel. There is a market for those feelings. Write these feelings down in as much detail as you can. We will add to this.

This example is instructive for the following reason. Even though you might love riding your bike, building a bike might not interest you because your work will be in manufacturing. Organizing races might not interest you because then your job would mostly focus on event planning. It is important to consider what your company will actually be *doing* on a daily basis. This must interest you.

2. How do you waste your time? If you are squirming in your seat right now thinking about how your answer involves snacking or spending too much time on Buzzfeed or Netflix, stop for a moment. Those answers are not useless.

Something about the activities on which you waste your time feels compelling to you. Let's use the Buzzfeed example. Most Buzzfeed articles depict common but often unspoken problems or emotions that large numbers of people experience, and portray them comically to humor the reader or put him or her at ease. So if you find that you waste time on Buzzfeed or something similar, what kind of articles do you typically read, and how do they make you feel? What specific tactics or triggers do those articles use that create those emotions in you?

If this specific example relates to you, please find five to ten articles or recordings that have appealed to you strongly and analyze what made them so powerful. Which specific sentences, images, or snippets evoked a response? Write them down. Once you have done that, look for commonalities. Do they bring you surprise? Do they relieve stress? Do you feel better about yourself, or possibly less self-conscious, as a result of reading, watching, or listening to them? If this specific example does not relate to you, where do you waste your time? Analyze those activities. Look for patterns. There is a market for these feelings that can be delivered in many ways.

Lastly, when you waste time, what situations and emotions are you trying to avoid? Be very honest with yourself. Is it fear of failure, or possibly boredom? Are you scared of something else? The answers to this question are the most useful tools you have when you are coming up with business ideas. The reason is that most people tend to be even more interested in avoiding problems than they are in indulging in positive things. When you can solve someone's burning pain, you will be successful.

3. Now, we will get more specific about the kinds of problems you wish to solve. Generally, this tends to mirror aspects of your life. Think of the many challenges you have faced in your life, and what made them so difficult. During those times, which of the six human needs were missing? Even small problems can inspire profoundly successful businesses. If you could have had solutions to any of them, what would they be? Would you be interested in providing solutions to these problems for other people?

If you wish to think more broadly, what problems in the world bother you most intensely? It is very easy to find inspiration, as the media is full of bad news. But on the positive side, problems can give you many great ideas. Write down what problems bother you the most. After doing that, research why these problems exist and map them out. *Actually do this exercise.* You will often be surprised at how seemingly unrelated the causes of problems can be to their outcomes, and how many commonalities exist.

As an example, I have done this exercise with climate change. In nearly every contributing factor to climate change (such as deforestation, agriculture, rise in carbon-intensive energy usage, etc.), unsustainable population growth due to extreme poverty was a primary contributor. The fact that extreme poverty showed up so many times made me realize that if I wanted to address climate change, I would need to further investigate and develop clean solutions for ending poverty. Similarly, the factors that show up the most frequently in your research will help you to direct your focus.

How to Discover Your Passions

Identifying Your Skills: Immersion

What are your natural talents? Think about this on a deeper level. Even if a skill seems as though it would be unprofitable (such as folding clothes), consider that you have other innate traits that enable that skill. For instance, if you are good at folding clothes, perhaps you have an eye for perfection, or you have a sense for the order in which tasks need to be carried out to produce the results you want, or you are skilled with your hands. This is what you are looking for.

As an example, I happen to be very good at probability because I identify patterns and understand them deeply. This allows me to see patterns in human psychology, behavior, and in all other areas of life. The ability to see patterns is profoundly useful in many ways, such as predicting future events (such as market trends) and understanding persuasion. So know that whatever skills you have extend well beyond those tasks. Try to identify the traits that make you so talented.

You will never know what you are good at until you try new activities for yourself. You will also not know how much you can improve until you work at something. Therefore, it is critical that you experience a variety of new things to learn about yourself. Make it a point to try at least one new activity each week that expands you, such as an improv comedy class or a horseback-riding lesson. Purchase a book of puzzles. Try something that involves persuasion, influence, or connection. Then try things that force you to be strategic. Approach these activities with curiosity and never take your failures personally, especially when you are trying something new. Instead, use these activities to identify your talents.

There is usually a lot of overlap between your natural talents and what you enjoy. These are the skills on which you must try to capitalize. There are many aspects of running a business, not all of which may be things that interest you or suit your skill set. Although you can usually hire out or build a team with complimentary skills, you will need to identify what you are good at and what you are honestly willing to do.

If you are looking for another great resource to help you to determine your skills, we recommend the StrengthsFinder test by Gallup.

Generating Ideas

To review, you have identified the feelings that you want to help your customers to eliminate, the feelings that you want to bring to your consumers, what you enjoy doing, and your natural talents. Now that you have done your background work, it is time to reverse engineer potential solutions.

Remember that your business does not have to address all the items in your lists. You have your whole life to start more businesses later. With that in mind, first identify specific industries that you enjoy (such as food, engineering, gaming, etc.). Identify one or several core problems from your list that mean the most to you. Research other companies or organizations that are working to eliminate those problems. Look across industries. What are their products, services, strategies, and business models? What is involved in setting up these enterprises? Let's consider a couple examples.

1. I have a friend, Leanne, who cares intensely about animal welfare and wanted to alleviate their suffering in factory farms. She spent years in seemingly unrelated careers: developing grassroots marketing strategies at Sittercity.com and for other companies while modeling with Ford Models in Chicago and on contracts in Asia. However, each winter, she had struggled to find beautiful and effective vegan outerwear. In fact, there were no companies making flattering coats for cold weather.

Leanne recognized this gaping void in the market. Drawing on her skills in marketing, fashion, and entrepreneurship, Leanne embarked on an eight-month-long journey of research and development to finally launch a brand under the name Vaute Couture. Given her skills, knowledge, and passion for her mission, Vaute Couture was a perfect match for her. It has grown year after year.

2. A former colleague of mine studied computer science and economics but was extremely passionate about ending poverty. She worked to develop solar-powered lighting, but she ultimately realized that her mission was to empower women to become economically self-sufficient. Finally, she drew on her background in economics and her appreciation for design to employ some of the world's finest female artisans to create top-quality bags and acces-

sories. She has worked with several high-end retailers to sell her products. Her company affords the workers a high wage and a path to self-sufficiency.

Now, let's go through an example of coming up with a business idea using a fictitious list.

Perhaps the underlying problem you want to address revolves around the fear of aging. This can disrupt four of the six human needs: the sense of physical safety, significance, love, and stimulation or pleasure. Therefore on a psychological level, your business should help to restore one or more of these needs.

Aging brings many issues. These can include problems such as loss of beauty, weight gain, low energy, or the degeneration of cognitive functions. Initially, you will only address a narrow subset of these. Refer to your list of interests and talents. Perhaps you have a passion for beauty, enjoy creating things, and are skilled at researching. Then one possible option would be to create a very effective skincare line that targets wrinkles or discoloration.

If this idea appeals to you, research the industry. What are the barriers to entry? Who are your competitors and what do they offer? How successful are they? Look up their reviews on Yelp and other rating websites. What are people's comments and criticisms?

Pay special attention to negative reviews, as these are the areas to which your business can bring innovation and can differentiate itself.

How to Discover Your Passions

Do this exercise several times and come up with a variety of ideas. You can choose the one you like the most or even combine them. Once you have come up with an idea, you should start by testing it on a small scale. Testing is essential for showing you what will and will not work.

Testing Your Ideas

Once you have a business idea, you should test it out to see if it has a market. Determine your target market and speak with them. What are their pains, and how attractive do they find your solution? How much would they realistically pay for that? How much are they currently paying for similar products or services? Actively seek out oversights in your business model. What will be your challenges? When you discover these early on, you will save yourself a lot of miseries later on when you are managing a lot more people and capital.

If you intend to start a product-based business, research what goes into creating products and the current best products in class. Write to business owners and entrepreneurs to find out their challenges. Get as much experience as you can, doing what you intend to do later on. When you start prototyping, start small and gather as many opinions as you can. Over time, you will see that your business will become more cost-efficient as your volume increases.

As an example, I had been interested in starting a food product company. After surveying a number of successful food product creators, I discovered that they all took more or less the same path. Most of these entrepreneurs started small in their own kitchens and initially sold their products at local fairs or open-air markets. As the demand for their products started to grow, they sought out investors to acquire commercial kitchens while working to get their products in as many stores as they could. As their revenues increased, they grew their supply to match their demand. However, the time and money involved in starting such a business was too great of a commitment for me at the time. I had larger priorities and other personal goals, such as travel, which would have been impossible had I started a product line at that point.

In the same way, if you take the time early on to determine whether a business is right for you, then you will be able to proceed with certainty that you have made the right decision. You will be much more committed to your business' success when you are certain that you care about it.

Multiple-Business Confusion Syndrome

What do you do if you have too many ideas? First, remind yourself that you are not limited to one business over the course of your life. You have time. The best entrepreneurs are decisive and committed to their tasks at hand. If you are just starting to decide what you want, write down all your ideas and honestly evaluate which of them mean the most to you. In particular, mark the ones that are absolute necessities for you and which ones you would be willing to forego if needed. In general, if two ideas seem equally important, choose the one that requires the least capital upfront and will allow you to grow the fastest (such as an online business). You can reinvest the earnings that you create from your businesses into new businesses if you choose.

If you are caught between two ideas – one of which is easy and inexpensive but means less to you than the costly one –honestly evaluate how long you would be willing to wait to start each business. Decide whether the easy idea is something you would be willing to put off in the meantime. This could mean that financial success would come much later. On the other hand, if you start the easier business first, you could have more money earlier on.

Lastly, when you decide on an idea, become very committed to it. Research the best strategy given your circumstances, and stick to your plan. You will be most the successful when you are laser focused and not confused or thrown off-course by hurdles that come your way (because they *will* come).

Most of all, remember that you have the power to get through anything because you are powerful beyond measure.

Chapter 3: The Shift

"Your thoughts are the rudder that steers your life. For every thought that you are having, there are trillions of potential thoughts that you aren't having. By sitting each day and contemplating goals, intentions and visions we are able to grab that rudder and steer the ship into new territories of greatness." –Tom Cronin

Shifts are catalyzed by an event or a series of events that allow individuals to change the course of their journeys, personally and professionally. But it should take much more than a simple shift in affinity for a position to inspire you to quit your job. In fact, your entire mental framework and your actions should align with that initial mindset change before you jump ship. When you have seen the signs, listened to the whispered hints and have felt the intuitive kick in the gut, you will know it is time to move forward.

The Shift

My shift first started knocking on my mind's door around eight months into my newly appointed position within the entertainment industry.

Up until that point, I was very grateful for the job. All my projects were fresh, challenging, and heavily focused on our company's diverse movie and TV properties. And I was continuing on the road to Hollywood stardom that I had begun two years prior. I was living the dream!

But by the 8-month mark, I started to realize that I wanted more variety, ownership, and fulfilling work. I began to wonder if I had made the right decision about what I was supposed to do with my life. My internal struggle had begun.

Eventually my boss and I had a meeting in which I asked her to do a midyear review with me. During our chat, I told her that I wanted more, and guess what I got? Much more. I was given greater tasks and duties in overseeing multiple people and engaging with even more individuals on the C-level all the way to the very top.

With my newly appointed tasks, I continued to go above and beyond, smash my benchmarks and become a go-to man in my department and company. During that initial period, I thought, 'life is pretty cool.'

From the exclusive VIP Hollywood Parties to the hands-on action with some of the year's biggest movies, it served as a momentary Band-Aid that helped me to keep up my enthusiasm.

But the truth started to re-emerge when the mornings that I woke up feeling irritated started to outnumber the mornings I awoke with anticipation and enthusiasm for work. Although my job kept me very busy, I was not content; my job did not light me on fire. And without that fire – that passion and a burning desire doing something I truly loved – there was no way I could ever forgive myself if I did not start taking bolder steps towards my dreams.

I started to crave a way out, but I was also afraid to let everyone around me down, including my parents, coworkers, and friends. After all, being a big shot and working in Hollywood and making millions of people laugh was my end-all, be-all goal. How could I simply just give up on something that I shared as my dream with so many people for such a long time?

As the days progressed, which then turned into weeks and then a few months, I started to experience this gripping feeling more and more as dissatisfaction played in my head. But I still showed up to work with my mask on, always happy and smiling.

In March of that year, the Universe started to push something in my direction. It came in the form of a twenty-five day, ten-country Personal Development cruise happening that December. When I first received the email, I immediately closed out my browser after seeing "25 days" because I knew there was no way that my job was going to allow me to take off that much time. A few days later I got another notification from a college buddy about the cruise. I turned down the offer. But within the next two to

The Shift

three weeks, I received several more notices about this cruise from a number of different friends.

Was my life trying to tell me something?

What eventually caught my attention was that none of the friends who sent me the offer knew each other. They had been sending me information on this cruise completely independently. I finally began to realize that I might have been hearing about this cruise for a reason. So instead of automatically thinking that it would cost too much or that I would never get enough time off, I started to redirect my mindset to allow this cruise to be a possibility.

Gradually I accepted this idea as an investment in myself. I searched for ways to pay for the cruise. I strategized about how I could approach my boss about taking so much time off at once and how to tell my family that I would be out of the country for Christmas.

Each step led to the next, and before long everything fell into place. It even turned out that since I had not taken a sick day since I started this job, I had just enough time off available to go on the cruise.

Before I knew it, I was stepping onto the boat to begin our Enrichment Voyage. This experience initiated my shift. It took many knocks on the door for me to wake up and realize a shift was taking place at all!

Had I not made the mental connections, I might have missed my opportunity.

The Two-Week Notice

Graduation was coming up fast and like many college students, I had no idea what I was going to do afterward. I was tirelessly networking and applying for jobs in my major's field, but getting rejected from every one. I could not understand why. I was doing everything that I had been told would bring me success. I was at the top of my class, participated in extracurricular activities and had a plethora of internship experiences. What was the disconnect that was keeping me from being hired?

As I interviewed more, I began to see a trend. I was not speaking the same language as my interviewers were. I spoke to them about passion, destiny, traveling the world and impacting humanity. They spoke to me about profit maximizing, company loyalty, long hours, and climbing the corporate ladder. It was no wonder these companies did not perceive me as a viable employee. They were looking for a company man who would sign onto their vision, but I already had a vision of my own and was committed to creating it.

The Shift

I persevered with the interviews even as I noticed this trend. Then one day I was turned down for a job because I forgot to bring a pen to the interview, which apparently made me look unprofessional. At that point, I decided I had had enough. It was time to make some drastic changes.

After searching for inspiration for weeks on end to attempt to figure out what was next, I came across a quote from Gandhi that said, "The best way to find yourself is to lose yourself in the service of others."

Immediately upon digesting that quote, I knew what I had to do as I had been subconsciously thinking of moving to New York City to volunteer for the summer for Dream Careers. After experiencing such a radical shift in my life as a participant two summers prior, I knew that I could facilitate the same type of transformation for students as a staff member. My mind was set, and I packed my bags to New York City to volunteer for ten weeks.

One of the biggest takeaways I had that summer was the reinforcement that I felt called to a career that positively impacts the lives of others. Every single day that summer I woke up inspired and excited to go to work because I was making other people's lives better. And I could not imagine a career that did anything else.

When I thought about this 'dream career' I would start after my volunteer experience ended, I questioned what I loved doing as a child when I was completely innocent and excited. How could that passion as a child be put towards a career that served others?

My answer: the sports industry.

As the summer volunteer opportunity ended and I moved back to my hometown of Pittsburgh, I set out to pursue a career I had always dreamed of but never had the courage to launch.

With no relevant work experience to back up my dream, I set off to land employment before December hit and my first student loans were due.

In this process, I did everything imaginable to land employment. I was working two unpaid internships, working part time for the Pittsburgh Steelers and going on an endless amount of coffee dates to network.

All of this moxie, 60 plus hours a week of minimum wage or free labor paid off as I found employment in the sports industry within three months. This was something almost completely unheard of as most people go years attempting to find a job in that industry.

My "dream" of working in sports had been achieved, and I thought I had found happiness.

I was wrong.

It took less than two months for me to realize that working for somebody else simply was not for me. This was a radical shift for me, especially since I had just finished college and had spent the last four years looking forward to exactly that kind of work situation. But the more I thought about it, the more I realized it was true.

In the back of my mind, I knew exactly what my end goal was for my career: run a six-figure business, travel the world, work wherever I wanted and push humanity forward. I had envisioned this lifestyle after reading the *4 Hour Workweek* and reading blogs of individuals living this exact type of lifestyle like Scott Dinsmore of *Live Your Legend*. This career path caught my eye for two reasons: freedom and happiness.

But I had two immediate problems. First, I did not know what my role would be, what work I would do or what business I would start. Second, I had just started my new job, and I did not yet have the preparation or the financial resources to leave. I was 23, broke, staring down my student loans, and facing what felt like insurmountable odds. As much as I wanted to strike out on my own right then, it just did not make sense yet.

So for the moment I stayed where I was, but I started planning my escape immediately. Social media had always come as second nature to me, so I decided to hone that skillset as a possible foundation for my own business.

I came to realize that I could use my social media skills and knowledge of new technology to help improve brands' communication strategies.

One of the top ways I learned how to build my business on the side was by working with a mentor. For me, my mentor was Andrew Hewitt, the Founder of GameChangers 500, a network of the world's top 500 for-benefit organizations.

I began helping his startup with social media marketing as the first company in my portfolio of case studies. Within only a short period, we had nearly doubled every major metric on Facebook and Twitter. This included number of fans, reach, and engagement levels.

While it seemed impossible to find the time at first, I spent every waking moment honing my skill set, working with GameChangers 500, and preparing to launch my own company (now known as No Typical Moments). This meant that that my car rides to work, post work hours, Friday nights, and entire weekends were spent in dedication to this goal. I believed that incremental steps would add up to massive gains over weeks and months.

As the season progressed at the sports team, however, I began to feel as if I was living in two separate realities. There was the 9-5 job and then there was the side hustle that represented possibility, hope and my desire for entrepreneurship. Whenever I worked on No Typical Moments, I felt more alive, directed, passionate, and happy.

By contrast, my job was leaving me completely unfilled, unhappy and depressed. I was making income below the poverty line, living in a rundown part of town and working over 70 hours a week, leaving barely any time or money to devote to No Typical Moments.

The Shift

What was more, I could not reconcile my values with the way the company was being run. For example, my employer hosted a country concert on June 16. From a revenue standpoint, the concert was a success, meaning it brought in more money than it cost to put it on. But from a personal standpoint, the concert was a difficult experience. Fans were having sex in the bathrooms or the stands. Many of these fans left the stadium drunk and drove home. We even had a drunken fan almost run over a staff member as he was driving away. I thought to myself, "What if a fan killed somebody on his way home? Even worse, what if multiple fans did the same thing because they attended our event?" Even though individuals have the choice to do whatever they want with their lives, I felt like I had helped to facilitate that behavior. I left the concert feeling completely disheartened.

As the weeks wore on, the sensation inside my belly to do something more meaningful with my life grew stronger and stronger. I believed from the bottom of my heart that No Typical Moments was this answer, but I was still lost as to how I could start a company with no revenue, business plan or savings. This unfulfilled desire, combined with my difficulties at work, began to take a toll on my health. I started to have anxiety attacks at night and even had to consciously prevent myself from fainting in the office.

As August began, I once again decided I had had enough. I made the decision that no matter what, I would quit my job to start No Typical Moments. Regardless of whether I had prospective customers, I would go for it. I knew what

No Typical Moments could do for its clients because of the metrics I had produced for GameChangers 500, and I felt that if I did not do it, somebody else would. Why could it not be me? For my entire life, I had been waiting for other people to give me permission to feel good about myself. For once, why could I not stand up for myself and do what I believed I was supposed to do?

So with these bold desires to change the world with an idea that had no formal business plan, no clients, and no revenue, I left what I had deemed as my dream job. I took the $6,000 I had to my name and moved back home.

Sometimes, the universe sends you clues. Other times it lights your pants on fire.

After I had finished at MIT, I was nowhere near ready to take on a lifestyle brand of my own. Like a good girl, I felt I should have a few years' experience at a large firm and some time to discover what I really wanted. So I moved away from my amazing circle of friends in Boston to join a Fortune 100 engineering firm. I would become a process engineer where I hoped to use my knowledge of nano-technology. I felt that in doing so, I would be using my skills and training to leave my mark on the world.

My entry into the real world was the worst shock I had ever received. I was put onto the nightshift at my new job and was told that I would have to "work my way up" before I could see the light of day. Being nocturnal quickly turned me into a miserable, comatose zombie. Every night I fought with all my strength to stay awake but always ended up on the brink of passing out. Eventually, I would sneak outside past the parking lot's resident skunk and attempt to take a nap in my car, desperately hoping that nobody would call me. Within two minutes, my phone would invariably go off, and I would have to go back inside.

The parking lot was always full of sleeping employees. One time I had gone to my car in a fit of exhaustion, but within three minutes I was disrupted by loud snoring sounds coming from the man in the truck across from me. Of course, none of this was allowed, and the rules were very rigid. The job itself was so boring that my ears perked up when my cubicle neighbors began discussing health insurance and mortgages. Nearly all the employees were aware of how dry their jobs were, but everyone seemed to have a way of dealing with it.

One friend of mine would hurriedly minimize his 1996 edition of Pinball Express when he heard my footsteps, but as I walked by, he would feel relieved that I was not his boss and resume playing. A few people camped out in the cafeteria and passed the time with hourly burgers or Lay's potato chips. Most would just rationalize their jobs by saying that they were too old to do something different.

In contrast to the role described to me at my interview, none of my MIT education, or even innate common sense, ended up playing a role in what I was doing. To add to this, I was one of very few women and probably the only young person there. Working in a sea of old men made me feel like a rotting banana in a room full of fruit flies. Even wearing a cleanroom onesie, which has the power to make Adriana Lima look like a sack of potatoes, did not help to address this issue.

One of my male friends would help me by sharing his experiences. He was a little shorter than me and had long, flowing blonde hair. He told me that when he was new, other employees would see his beautiful hair from the back and whistle at him. He would turn around and flash his bearded smile. The resulting embarrassment was permanent. But I did not have such a luxury.

Like the majority of my coworkers, my health fell severely out of balance, and I became deeply depressed.

Then four months after I started my job, four people independently suggested that I should start a business after seeing my writing about self-help. The experience worked some magic on me. The thought of starting a business was foreign to me at the time but it gave me so much hope. From that point on, I became even more frantic to leave my job. I thought about the kind of lifestyle I wanted to create and what I had learned about myself from my job. I realized that freedom, self-care, location flexibility, creativity, and contribution were essential to my happiness.

Understanding these lifestyle values about myself was my shift. And once I had figured those out, through some fortuitous events I soon started gaining clarity on what I would create to form that lifestyle for myself. I became more deeply involved in personal growth and emotional mastery. This inspired me to create a lifestyle brand around healthy eating and quality of life. I knew I would later go on to create other enterprises in various fields. After eighteen months of starting my job, I pulled the plug on it, took a few months off, and made the deep-dive into writing, researching, and coaching.

Now, I have some questions for you: Do you have ambitions that shake your soul and keep you up at night? Do you want to transform the world? Do you feel trapped in a job you hate and do not know how to leave? If you answered "yes" to any of these, then follow us to the next chapter and let us show you how.

Chapter 4: How to Quit

"If you are ready, go." –Momma Echols

It is not easy to leave a job, especially when you are reminded of the insecurity and inconsistency that you might experience. But remember that it is much harder to work for the rest of your life, doing things that you dislike and helping build someone else's dreams.

Although my initial shift began after nine months at work, I did not quit until a few months after that. It is one thing to think about doing something and an entirely different one to actually do it.

When all my feelings of fulfillment began to leak away from me, I decided to act.

My time came when my thoughts of moving forward came more and more frequently as the universe started to open up new doors for me. There was no denying the fact that Paolo Coelho's quote from the Alchemist was proving to be true in my life at that time: "when you want something, all the universe conspires in helping you to achieve it." The more my mindset shifted and the more new opportunities revealed themselves, the readier I felt to move in a new direction.

But I could not just drop everything and walk away. At least, I did not want to because I greatly respected the people with whom I worked. During the three weeks leading up to the cruise I talked about in the previous chapter, I had to work my butt off to complete my outstanding projects and all the other work I would miss when I was gone. It was not easy, especially during the holiday rush, but I got it all done.

Just before I was scheduled to walk out of the studio and onto the cruise ship, my bosses called me into their office...and promoted me.

I was stunned. I knew I had been doing good work, but over the last eight months my mindset had shifted so much that I was already halfway out the door to the Caribbean to start the cruise. I did not expect a promotion—especially not right before I left for my big personal growth vacation!

I was happy, but I was also confused. Was I being promoted in recognition of my work? Or was it because my bosses could sense my shifting mindset and wanted to keep me around? I wrestled with that dilemma for a while on the way to the airport, and then tried to forget about it in the whirlwind of my retreat.

After a few days aboard the MV Explorer, I enrolled in Rapid Results Retreats, which was led by Jairek Robbins, who is the son of the #1 Results and Performance Coach in the world, Anthony Robbins. On the first day we were asked to go around the class and introduce ourselves. This is exactly what I said:

"Hi, my name is Alex Echols. I work in entertainment, I know who I am and I know where I am going in life. I don't think I will be around these sessions much, but I thought I'd come by to check it out." And I proceeded to sit down (earning a reputation as a cocky prick as I did so – oops!).

And then something interesting and incredible happened. After the second session, I became hooked. The Rapid Results Retreat was focused on "discovering yourself while you discovered the world." What a fitting title!

I discovered much more about myself in twenty-five days than I had in many years. I had never cried so much until that experience. There was a time when I wrote in my journal just how much I hated being on the retreat, but something deep down within knew that it was best for me.

Most of my tears came up during an exercise we did where I was asked about who I wanted love from the most growing up? Initially, I thought it was a pretty easy answer: my peers, my mom...everyone.

But as Jairek and I dug deeper, he helped me reach the very powerful realization that the person I wanted love from the most was my father. He had never been much of a communicator, and I do not think he truly understood how different I was growing up. Jairek's coaching opened my eyes but also hit a lot of sensitive nerves. Ironically enough, that was just the beginning of much more. During our coaching sessions, Jairek and the rest of our group helped me work through much more. I broke through wooden boards as I broke through mental blocks and bullshit stories I had been living with for many years.

I felt something shifting inside me.

My life was evolving, and questions about work finally resurfaced. Before this experience, I felt ready to resign from my job the minute I stepped off the cruise ship and pursue a more purposeful path within personal growth and development. As our retreat group talked about discovering our worth, planning for the future with our biggest goals, and unlocking our true potential, I went on to have multiple conversations over the next few days with three individuals that helped me think through my thoughts about leaving my job over the next few days.

My friend's mother, a fellow retreat mate, and a fellow passenger on the ship all said the same thing:

"You are a really passionate person and it seems like you really want to go, but can I suggest that you stay there just a bit longer before you make your final decision? Just be patient, give it some time and go with the flow."

Initially, this was not what I wanted to hear. Generally the things that piss us off the most are the most important lessons that we need to hear in those moments. While I thought I had my mind made up, these outside opinions were influencing me to rethink my plans. Should I listen to them or should I not? Did what they said have valid points or no? What should I do? And if I choose to stay for some time, for how long would I stay? My decision was to return to my job until I just intuitively knew it was my time to go – not because something pissed me off or made me uncomfortable – but only if I could truly feel it was my time to bounce forward.

So I did. I returned to work and embraced the flow, trusting that when it truly was the right time to leave, I would know. For the next three months, I worked even harder and felt more alive than ever before. Keeping my mother's and friends' words of encouragement in the back of my mind, I began to align my intention with my actions of wanting more.

Then, about two months later, another opportunity came across my desk: to return to the MV Explorer for another voyage, this time throughout Europe and the Mediterranean for fifty-two days. Earlier in the book, I touched on how much international travel reframed my entire outlook on life, so not only did I take this as a sign, I looked at it as massive nudge. But first, I had a very important decision to make. I knew I had to decide between the voyage and my job. I could not do both.

How to Quit

I reached out to the same three people who offered me their opinions earlier (as well as a few others), and with remarkable synchronicity they all told me the same thing: "if you're ready, go."

By this time, my bosses knew a change was coming for me as I boldly began to speak of dreams bigger than the entertainment industry. I was now speaking more about my dreams to inspire and motivate the masses. They could sense that my urge to set sail around the world had returned, and despite a lot of initial reluctance, they wanted nothing but the best for me – which was an absolute blessing. We were all very thankful for the opportunity to work together, but it was my time to go.

While I knew I would miss them, my Hollywood lifestyle, and the amazing experiences I had had, I also knew that my life was shifting in a new, expanded direction.

So I went. And I have not looked back.

The Two-Week Notice

In the quest for freedom from your job, you may experience a struggle between your heart and mind. Your heart will tell you that leaving your job is what you were meant to do. On the other hand, the logical part of you is assessing whether it makes sense to do so. Can you really withstand the emotional strain of the leaving?

There is *never* a good time to quit a job and build your own company. You can *always* find an excuse. Right now, perhaps the reason is a looming student loan and your lack of experience. But when you are 30 (or 40, or 60) you will have another laundry list of excuses such as saving for retirement, putting a down payment on a house or spending time with your kids.

As explained by the bestselling author of *Love Yourself (Like Your Life Depended On It)* Kamal Ravikant: "Entrepreneurship is just an expression of you." What feels right in your heart tends to be the correct answer. And if it is not, you can detach your happiness from the results and learn from the experience.

Internally, I felt out of flow for a very long time at my job. I woke up each day feeling like I was trapped in two separate realities. There was the No Typical Moments reality where my dreams, happiness and company awaited me.

On the other hand, my job made me feel like my soul was being sucked out of me. I did not feel like I was myself, and I could barely recognize the person that I had become. I was constantly stressed out, in a bad mood, was not intellectually stimulated and had no social life. This was the exact opposite way I had envisioned my life playing out through working in the sports industry. I did not think it would be all roses and unicorns, but I did not picture myself even getting to the point of not wanting to get out of bed in the morning to go to work. To add to that, I was making below the poverty line, stuck in a poverty stricken town and living in a college dorm room. It was not the ideal picture of how my life was going to play out.

Eventually, the feeling and longing of something more was too much for me to handle, and I decided that enough was enough. It was time to stand up for my beliefs and passions, step into my greatness and serve others.

I felt so-called to this idea that I left my job with nothing but a dream. I had $6,000 saved up, no clients, no revenue stream, and no capital. I tucked my tail between my legs and moved back home. I set out to embark upon my personal legend and make the world a better place.

That said, I did not leave without a plan, nor did I impulsively quit one morning in an act of rage.

Sometimes you cannot take the time to design and carry out a months-long exit strategy – you may be fired, or your situation may be so intolerable you just have to get out *now* – but if at all possible I would recommend putting this kind of plan into action, which we have included at the end of this chapter. Regardless of your age or how long you have been in your current job, start by answering some of the following questions:

- If you woke up five years into the future and you were still at this company and job, would you be happy?
- Is your job contributing to your overall health and well-being?
- Why do you think you should start your own business?
- How would having your own company put you in a better position than you currently are?
- Will you still be happy even if your business fails?
- Are you willing to work on nights and weekends while your friends are out socializing?

Answer these questions, and consider the tips that we have included at the end of this chapter. These tips formed the backbone of my exit strategy. I spent several months working on them in preparation to leave my job and start my own company.

Your heart knows what you truly desire. It is now just a matter of listening to your intuition or and taking gradual action to prepare you to pursue that desire full-time.

How to Quit

Leaving my job did not feel right or make sense until fifteen months after I started. But much like Alex's situation, when I felt it was time to go the circumstances matched up to make it possible. Andrew and I were fortunate in that when we started thinking about leaving our jobs, we already knew what we wanted to do instead. But what if you do not know what you want to do yet? You recognize that your current job is not right for you, but that is as far as you have gotten. What now?

As Andrew mentioned, you should envision exactly what you want your life to look like. Strive towards this. Use our guide to help you find your passion, and do your homework. It will take time and effort to set up your own business, but knowing how you want to live will help you decide on the kind of business you want to start in the first place. We will talk a lot more about these thought processes in the next two chapters.

As a rule of thumb, you want to take advice from people whom you want to emulate — ideally, these are people who have already taken the kind of entrepreneurial leap you are getting ready to take. At the same time, be careful whom you ask for advice — especially friends or family members. Alex was fortunate enough to have a lot of family support, but not all of us are that lucky.

You might encounter a lot of opposition from friends and family. Many people are used to choosing security over the chance at what they truly want, (or do not know what they want at all!) and feel like doing anything else is unwise. If you are related to or friends with these people, they may feel the need to tell you, you are making a mistake. Consider their objections and be polite, but take their advice with a grain of salt. They mean well, but they do not share your values or dreams.

Many people will tell you to build your business on the side and then make the transition once your business is successful enough. However, this could be unrealistic for you. You might want to consider switching jobs to one that would more easily allow you to build your business concurrently.

Once you decide to quit, plan your time well. When I was still at my job, I focused so hard on my desperation to leave that I barely worked on my craft. I felt stuck, and the uncertainty of being successful on my own kept me from moving forward. But if I had given myself a set deadline by which I would leave and believed it, I could have relaxed in the knowledge of the outcome and actually moved forward.

Here are some important steps to get you started:

1. Set up a timeline. Pick a date and make an ironclad promise to yourself that you will leave by that time. Once you know just how much time you have left at your job, you will be able to set milestones for developing the business and preparing to leave.

2. Get healthy mentally and physically. It is easy to get bogged down by a job you hate, but know that your time will be limited. Treat yourself with love and prioritize yourself.

(*From Andrew*) A major breakthrough happened in my business when I started paying attention to my mental health. I started reading personal development books, meditating and eating healthier. In turn, I had greater sustained energy. We'll talk more about physical and mental health in a few more chapters.

3. Start saving money. You will likely need three times as much as you think. It is imperative to save pennies everywhere you can because you are going to need all of that money, and more, when you make the leap. This means cutting back on clothes, alcohol, and fancy nights out, and instead engaging in free activities, like hosting a community dinner, running, reading a book or meditating.

4. Meet people who are doing what you want to do. We cannot stress enough how important it is to start connecting with other like-minded entrepreneurs. These individuals are facing the same types of problems you are. Having them as friends will give you a sense of community. We will discuss this in a later chapter.

5. Find the time to work on your business before and after work. Every entrepreneur we have met who had a full-time job worked on his or her business as a "side project". This is very important so you can assess the validity of your idea, learn how passionate you are about the company, and enhance your current skill set.

6. Work intelligently. Once you know that you will be quitting, you might be able to minimize the effort that you expend at your job so that you can focus more on yourself and your business. Do as much as you need, but keep the big picture in mind.

7. Lay down the fundamentals. Know exactly what business you want to start (refer to Chapter 2) and start making progress towards it. Pick all the low-hanging fruit first, such as setting up your LLC, printing your business cards, and having your website completed. If you have all of this done in advance, you can hit the ground running once you quit.

8. Use this time to market yourself. For most businesses, there is a period where the business is building visibility. However, if you can do this while you are still working, you will put yourself at an advantage once you leave.

9. Read. Even though your formal education may be over, you are in a continual state of learning. This does not just mean learning to understand that latest and greatest sales tactic. It means expanding yourself and enhancing your emotional intelligence. Even if you do not like to read, there are many amazing podcasts out there like *The School of Greatness* with Lewis Howes. In addition, audiobooks are easier than ever to buy, rent or download.

10. Attend conferences. The entrepreneurs you are dying to meet are not hanging out at happy hour networking events. These typical events do not create the same type of magic as an event specifically geared at personal or business growth. Start to attend events like Burning Man, Awesomeness Fest or World Domination Summit even before you launch a company. If those epic retreats are a bit out of your budget, make them next year's savings goals and attend smaller ones like Live Your Legend Regional Events, Toastmasters, and university & co-working hosted entrepreneurial events.

11. Evaluate your environment. Is your current location going to give you the greatest chance to succeed? Can you endure the cold winter months or would a tropical location better serve the advancement of your business? If moving is not practical right now, can you incorporate it into your long-term exit strategy or plan to do it in a certain number of months from your quitting day?

12. Always have a back-up plan. Entrepreneurship is, by definition, uncertain. Things will often go against all planning, so you never want to jeopardize yourself. Know how much your expenses are each month (or planning period), and always have enough to last you at least two to three months, so that in case you need to get another bridge job, you will have enough time.

Chapter 5: Transitioning Out

"Never cut what you can untie." –Robert Frost

Let's face it: most people do not wake up one day and say to themselves "I feel like quitting today! I think I am going to do it." Generally, other circumstances, events and triggers initiate such decisions.

For example, you might feel a strong desire to work on a project or cause that is bigger than you. Once you identify what that cause is and your role in it, you must lay the groundwork to make it happen. Let's consider an example.

Salman Khan was initially working as a hedge fund analyst when he started using online tools to tutor his cousin Nadia in math, which inspired his strong interest in education. After he created a YouTube account in November 2006, fans started to rave over Khan's educational vide-

Transitioning Out

os, and he began to realize that he could impact millions of lives through education.

The popularity of the videos and the many positive comments on his YouTube channel inspired Khan to quit his job in late 2009 to start Khan Academy (Temple).

Khan was strategic in his implementation. He first consulted his family about the decision. He described this endeavor to his wife as the "highest social return that one could ever get. With so little effort on my own part, I can empower an unlimited amount of people for all time. I can't imagine a better use of my time."

Khan started small and progressively built his organization. He acquired significant backing from donors such as the Bill & Melinda Gates Foundation, the Lemann Foundation, Google, and others.

Now, Khan Academy has gained global popularity, and over 4 million instructional exercises are completed on his platform daily (Sen).

What can be learned from this? The most important lesson is that planning is essential.

Once you have made the decision to leave your job, there are many logistical issues to consider while you are preparing to make the change. In particular, you will need some way of supporting yourself immediately after you leave while you build up revenue from your new business.

Savings and Bridge Jobs

You might be able to get paid to leave your job – that is, finding a way to leave with a separation package. This might not always be possible, but this scenario is worth investigating. If your company is looking to downsize, you might be able to volunteer to be let go.

If you feel that the job is a poor fit for you, then neither you nor your company benefits from you working in that role, and you can similarly approach your supervisor(s) with a proposal to leave, allowing them to find a replacement that fits the company better. In doing either of these things, you might be able to negotiate a separation package that would allow you several months of buffer to provide for yourself.

If you are unable to leave immediately, determine exactly how long you are willing to stay, and be reasonable with how much money you can save weekly or monthly. Work backward, and commit to a hard deadline by which you will leave your job or transition into alternative employment. Budget and save as much as you can, and if you have loans, consider paying less towards them or even just the minimum amount so that you can comfortably leave. Understand that you have the intention of becoming financially successful, so paying a little extra interest on your loans might be worth the flexibility and peace of mind you gain from being able to leave an unsuitable job sooner.

Alternately, you might be able to find a less stressful job within your company that allows you to build your business alongside your work. Sometimes it is easier to transfer within your own company than to find something external. If you decide to take this option, it will still be necessary for you to budget and save so that you have the ability to leave.

Another option is to look for a more flexible job outside of your company. This can be a surprisingly attractive option. Look for remote jobs that allow you to work on your own schedule from anywhere. A growing number of companies offer this. Lastly, you might decide that you can form a partnership, or commit to one or more part-time jobs that give you flexibility of schedule while keeping you afloat financially.

Part-Time Jobs

If you decide to go down the route of finding one or more part-time jobs, consider what makes building your business too difficult to do while staying at your current job. If it is the number of hours or the inflexibility of your work schedule, look for jobs that allow you freedom of time or the ability to pick your hours. Or maybe your current job stresses you out so much that you do not have the energy even to think about your business. If this is the case, think of what you would enjoy doing that will not rob you of mental bandwidth. The best-case scenario would be to find part-time work that complements your business.

In addition, there are many jobs that you can find which arise as-needed and for which you can get paid by the hour. For instance, you can join a cab service such as Uber or Lyft that notify you when someone needs a ride, and you can choose to accept or decline based on your schedule at that moment. You might be able to work as a caretaker or find odd jobs online, or through local venues that post ads for people's services.

Lastly, there are many ways that you can save money or get a little extra:

- Rent out your car or living space. For instance, you can list an extra bedroom on Airbnb to make money with very little added time.

- Monetize your workout! Especially if you are in the field of coaching or wellness, you can gain exposure by teaching classes.

- If you are a US resident and you will be leaving your job soon, you can declare yourself as "tax exempt". This is a smart decision that will give you some extra security as you transition out.

Transitioning Out

- Once you are no longer employed, you can apply for nutrition assistance and thereby collect money through food stamps.

- If you have student loans, you can apply for unemployment deferment until you generate enough cash flow to start repaying your loans.

- For things like your website or other services that you might need which you do not wish to do on your own, find friends with whom you can barter or have them do at a lower cost. You can save a lot of money, as well as gain exposure by tapping into your own network.

- Lastly, sell your crap! Be honest about what you use, what you like, and what you need. Get rid of what does not serve you. It will not only expand your space, but you will have a little extra cash flow to keep you going.

Taking Your Leave

After you have consulted those whose advice you value the most and have decided you are ready to move forward, begin to talk yourself through what you are going to say to your boss during your resignation. Some jobs still require a formal letter of resignation, but for most companies these days, a verbal resignation will do. Here's a good example of what you could say:

"Thank you for agreeing to see me this afternoon. I would like to thank you so much for the incredible leadership and guidance you have provided me with. I have had an incredible experience here and have definitely learned a lot.

With that said, I feel ready to move forward and discover what else my professional career has in store for me. I will take everything I have picked up throughout my career here and will use it to serve humanity fairly and positively. I am excited about my upcoming travels and adventures – I am excited to see what's next.

Thank you for the amazing years and I look forward to sharing a glass of champagne with each of you at my farewell."

I would advise you to have the initial talk with your boss somewhere between 3-4 weeks before your final day.

Why 3-4 weeks?

Because you want to show to your bosses and team that although you are moving forward, that you still respect and care about the team enough to allow time to wrap up your current projects. On the other hand, giving 3-4

Transitioning Out

weeks of notice also means your bosses do not have too much time to throw loads of new projects your way before you leave.

Now that you have given your formal notice to your bosses and subsequently Human Resources to finalize the decision, it is the perfect time for you to:

1. Set up meetings and lunches with colleagues (the ones with whom you connected the most) to share the news of you moving forward, other opportunities that have presented themselves and to receive some nice words of encouragement before you go.

2. Work with your direct supervisors to ensure that you are handling all outstanding projects before you go. The last thing you want is to dump a bunch of work in your colleagues' laps. Be respectful of the fact that they will still be there after you leave.

3. For all the people that you could not find the time to grab lunch with, send them an email or message with the news and get their contact information to stay in touch with them after you have left.

If you want to go above and beyond before you leave, you can do these two things as well:

4. Find your replacement. Find someone that you know is skilled and experienced enough to replace you and suggest him or her to your bosses and to Human Resources. Think of past interns or temporary employees you either

managed or worked closely with. A person with whom you were particularly impressed is a good place to start looking for your replacement.

5. And finally, with 3-4 weeks left before your final day, you have time to connect with your coworkers to set up your going away bash and celebration. It is the perfect way to have a spectacular going away party, give a few remarks about moving forward, share some love with your coworkers and pop some champagne.

Now, who would not want to go out like that?

Section II

Nurturing the Entrepreneur

Chapter 6: Changing Tracks

Sometimes when you decide to leave a job that is not serving you, what you feel inspired to do next is completely different from the career path you just left. This can be exciting and exploratory, but it presents challenges as well. In this chapter, we will look at two of the most difficult questions you may run into during this transition: "Did I just waste years of my life?" and "This did not work, how do I find what does?"

You Do Not Have to Pursue What You Went to School For

Like many people, I grew up believing the role of a university education is to prepare people for their future jobs.

Therefore, pursuing practical majors in employable fields was the best (and only) path to take in college. But after a certain point, I noticed that a lot of the individuals outside of employable majors went on to own successful businesses or attended medical or law school. They seemed to have no feeling of being bound to finding a job in the field of their major. Meanwhile, I was in a stifling corporate job that never even asked me to use the skills I learned while studying engineering.

At the same time, I felt immensely guilty about devoting a few years to pursuing a venture that relied on the opposite half of my brain than the one I had used my entire life. As I eventually made the transition, I realized that this dilemma is very common—and not just in the minds of those changing tracks themselves. If you feel this conflict, this might help you.

In my opinion, the belief that an education or career path permanently defines a person is dangerous, particularly for someone who has never worked in a field before. How can you know what you want until you have tried something out for yourself? You can't. The average Millennial is projected to have fifteen to twenty jobs over the course of his or her lifetime. Changing career tracks is likely to be a natural consequence of this.

Let's reframe how we view schooling. It is traditional and still common to think of school as a means to a greater end (as I initially did): a job that pays well, security, and a generally comfortable life.

I believe your education was an end in itself. It taught you new ways of thinking and enriched your experience during the years that marked your transition into adulthood. It tested you, not just academically, but socially, and perhaps spiritually or physically. It gave you new perspectives on life, allowed you to meet different types of people, and exposed you to things that you would never have been able to see otherwise. Most likely, many of your best friends came from school. So regardless of what you studied, you learned and experienced a lot of important things in school.

Similarly, there were many aspects of life for which school did *not* prepare you. These might include financial planning, paying taxes, insurance structures, life skills, time management, food preparation, health and self-care, relationships, emotional mastery, and much more. Most importantly, most education programs do not emphasize self-discovery and finding your passion.

So did you waste several years and tens (or hundreds) of thousands of dollars getting a degree that you do not want to use anymore?

No way.

School was a formative experience that prepared you to be where you are right now. Even if it is hard to see exactly how that worked, be patient and trust that it did.

As Steve Jobs encouraged in his famous Stanford address, allow the dots to connect. And in the meantime, you know the new path you are on is the right one for you, so trust yourself and keep moving forward.

Changing Tracks

Know Your Value:
Capitalizing On All of Your Skills

Andrew was fortunate: when he left his job, he already had a very clear vision and plan for the business he wanted to start because he had already started it. Alex too had a pretty clear idea of where he was going. But when I first started thinking about leaving my job, I had some issues around my skill set to work through before I could figure out what I could do.

I was terrible at my job, which was very different from the work I did in school. It had no mathematics, which was a bad shock for me. I hated the monotony of routine, and I prefer to rely on logic rather than memorization. I watched my co-workers thrive in the corporate environment, and over time I began to wonder what was wrong with me. My confidence eroded, and I stopped believing in my own intelligence. It was not until I started creating again and coming up with ideas for other people's businesses that I realized that my problem was not that I lacked skills. My problem was that I was in the wrong kind of job, one that did not leverage the skills I had.

As we talked about in the school section, it is easy to believe only traditional jobs and courses of study can provide a viable return on investment. I often hear artists and humanitarians tell me that they wish they had an engineering-oriented mind, and that their lives would be so much easier if they did (probably because they feel they'd have steadier income). However, the skills that are traditionally lauded the most – such as book smarts or speed – are not *necessarily* the most valuable.

Rather, the main distinguishing factor of highly successful people is that instead of trying to make their skill set fit their job environment, highly successful people recognize what can be created using their talents and create a new environment for themselves where those skills are integral to success. In this section, I encourage you to look at your skills and passions – even the subtle ones that might be easy to overlook – and recognize that you can learn how to leverage any or even all of them.

For instance, if you love psychology, there are many ways to channel your interests and skills. You can excel at marketing, management, or consulting. You can help people in their personal lives by starting a practice as a coach, writing books, or creating audio or video recordings to share your insights. You can invent devices or applications to help people reduce their stress levels, boost their brainpower, improve their emotional states, or change destructive behavior. These are just a few ideas, but the possibilities are endless. As an entrepreneur, creativity is your currency.

This is what I mean by leveraging your skills and passions. With a little creativity, you can think of many uses for any skill that you might want to put to use. As long as you are able to fill a need, eliminate a problem, or redefine an existing product or practice for the better, you can succeed in business.

Chapter 7:
Entrepreneurial Depression

Disclaimer: This section is here to describe my experience with entrepreneurial depression and does not serve as professional or medical advice. If you are struggling with depression, it is important that you seek help from a trained professional.

You can read all you want to about how to start a business. However, the truth of the matter is that the emotional aspect of entrepreneurship is very difficult to comprehend until you have experienced it.

The first 90 days of starting No Typical Moments were the hardest three months of my life. I woke up, got told "no" in every sales meeting I had, went to bed, and repeated the process the next day. This cycle repeated itself every single day for three months straight.

I distinctly remember spending most of those three months being lost with how to land a customer. However,

The Two-Week Notice

I had some experience in college, canvassing for a political campaign and knew the process of going door to door for sales.

I ventured down to Oakland in Pittsburgh and went from business to business, attempting to persuade the owner to have a five-minute conversation with me. I would walk into a business with a preexisting survey so I could identify his businesses pain points and make suggestions on their current customer acquisition strategies. I surveyed over 30 organizations and was pushed out the door of every single one. Literally no company wanted to hear how I could create a solution to improve their bottom line.

Imagine if you risked your entire career and financial security to pursue what you believed in your heart to be your destiny, and it all came crashing down on you. Would it still be worth it?

For me, the answer was yes.

However, the emotional burdens of starting a company soon caught up with me in a way I never expected.

I was so focused on getting No Typical Moments off the ground that I was not eating. Even though I had moved back home, I was too proud to accept free meals from my parents. As a result, I was only consuming water and protein shakes, peanut butter sandwiches and coffee to power me through the day. On some level I knew this practice was not healthy, but between pride and preoccupation with the business, I did not give it much thought until one night I got a wake-up call.

As I began to get dressed for a dinner party with my parents, I accidentally fit into a pair of my sisters' pants. My sister is about 5 feet tall and barely over 100 lbs. I was 5 feet 8 inches and usually weighed around 145—I was pretty trim, but I had always been bigger than my sister! I realized I had dropped to under 135 pounds. I had lost 10 pounds in the first month of entrepreneurship.

If you have ever hit rock bottom, you know what it feels like to be utterly confused and lost, like you have let the entire world down. This particular chain of events made me hit rock bottom because I felt like a complete failure. For my entire life, the one thing I could always count on to get me out of sticky situations was my intellect. But in this situation, 'thinking' harder only made the situation worse. With this reasoning, I felt like if my own offering to the world, my intelligence, could not suffice, and that nobody would ever love me again.

This train of thought can result in a deepening depression where things just get worse and worse. However, I was not even aware of the fact that I was starting to become depressed because of how hyper-focused I was on my business. Some of the warning signs that I was becoming depressed included not wanting to hang out with my friends, not exercising and having barely any energy.

Maybe it was my warrior spirit telling me to get my shit together, or Stone Cold Steve Austin telling me he would whip my ass if I did not pick things up. Through mindfulness practices, reading and studying positive psychology I was able to rebuild my life.

For example, I bought a library card (which is free) and began renting books off the shelves on a daily basis. This included *The Power of Now* by Eckhart Tolle, *Unlimited Power* by Tony Robbins and *The Alchemist* by Paulo Coelho. I also started my days in a completely different manner. Previously, I went immediately to reading The NY Times or CNN to digest the previous day's news. But after reflecting on this, I realized that these news outlets put me in a poor mood immediately as the day started. Instead, I began to do something upon waking up that made me happy. This included working out, watching The Colbert Report or reading an inspirational blog.

It was through this daily practice that I heard a talk by Vishen Lakhiani called "Happiness is the New Productivity" that completely transformed my perspective. In this video, he talks about four states of flow:

1. Unhappy now and no vision of the future. This is the worst possible state to be in because you are depressed and have nothing to look forward to.

2. Happy now but no vision of the future. Many college students, and, in fact, much of society as a whole, tends to fall into this trap: we are happy now because we are partying, drinking, and enjoying temporary pleasures, but we have absolutely no clue how our future is going to unfold. We are living completely in the present moment because it is too challenging for us to envision anything different.

3. Unhappy now but massive visions of the future. This was how I felt back then. Many entrepreneurs find themselves in this position. We are not in stage 1 because we are always focused on the future. But our goals are so massive that they leave us miserable in the present moment because our reality has not caught up to us yet. We are constantly telling ourselves that we will be happy when XYZ happens.

4. Happy now with massive visions of the future. As Vishen articulated, this is the epitome of flow. You are happy now, *and* you have big goals for your future. Your happiness is detached from your goals. You do not become happy because you achieve your goals. You achieve your goals because you are happy.

After thoroughly digesting Vishen's talk for the next couple of weeks, why I had hit rock bottom started to make sense to me. I had such a massive vision of what No Typical Moments could become that it left me miserable in the present. I told myself that I would relax and be happy when I reached my goals. But it was actually the complete opposite. I needed to become happy right now. If I did not, my goals would never be realized because my self-worth would always be attached them.

My process of healing soon began. I decided to take a different approach to finding happiness than what is deemed logical by society. We are told that happiness can be found at the bar, in new clothes, by having sex or in a pill. I decided to take a different approach focused on discovering that happiness from within instead of through external forms. That's what felt right to me to rebuild myself into the person I imagined becoming when No Typical Moments was merely an idea. This man was self-confident, knew exactly what he wanted, went after what he desired and inspired others to be the best version of themselves.

I also took an unorthodox approach to how I would manage and build No Typical Moments going forward. I implemented a one for one model similar to the model pioneered by *a verynice design studio*. With every paying client we worked with, we would allocate pro-bono services to a non-profit organization. And with this renewed sense of purpose and direction, revenue started to increase. Imagine that: doing good was a good business decision!

The process of pulling myself out of this slump was by no means a simple answer. It took days, weeks and months to feel like myself again. It was through the combination of daily practices that compounded over time and helping others that solved this problem for me. If you are in a situation that sounds like this, I would advise creating an answer that feels right to you. Whatever you decide though, make sure that you seek help, give yourself time and treat your body and mind with care.

Chapter 8: Mindset, Self-Trust and Emotional Health

"Start your day with meditation, gratitude and movement for all the great, unseen blessings that will occur today." –Christine Bullock

Depression deserved its own chapter because it is a serious issue that will keep you from moving forward in your business and your life. If you struggle with depression, feel free to refer to that chapter as often as you need to in your journey.

Now we are going to talk more broadly about your entrepreneurial mindset. We have introduced you to this idea in the chapter about the shift.

Now it is time to dig deeper. We will also explore trusting yourself and maintaining emotional health through the ups and downs of becoming a successful entrepreneur.

Anything is possible in life, right?

Well, not exactly. Anything and everything is possible ... *if* you have the right mindset about it, trust yourself, and are emotionally healthy.

No great entrepreneur has ever become very successful without first believing that he or she could accomplish a great feat. In fact, many entrepreneurs (including us) think that good emotional health comes before skill, connections, resources, self-confidence.

Vishen Lakhiani of Mindvalley has said: "...things move smoothest – business, family life, friendships, my goals – when I am in the space of being happy with the present while having a positive expectation for the future."

Becoming an entrepreneur without a foundation of self-trust is like gearing up to begin the longest and toughest bike ride of your life, and not believing that you can actually finish. It just will not work that way.

So how do you develop this mindset of belief in yourself? In our experience and that of other successful entrepreneurs, there are many different options to increase your level of self-trust and emotional health. Here are some that we have found to be great assets.

Invest in Your Mind

Years ago, closer to when I was about 18 or 19, I started sharing my thoughts on a self-run blog. It started off with posts of 100-200 words of me babbling along. But after a while, it started to evolve into more of a personal development blog in which I shared experiences that I was going through as a college student and later as a professional, and the lessons I was learning along the way. As I began to share more and more, the blog picked up traction and was shared amongst thousands and thousands of readers. Looking back, I thought I knew it all – I was offering so much advice on personal development without taking more of it myself. I was giving, but not receiving.

And then I discovered how leaders coached others on integrating personal development practices into their professional lives. I am referring to people like Tony Robbins, Abraham Hicks, and other personal development (PD) giants of whom I had heard in passing, but did not know much about until my Enrichment Voyage Rapid Results Retreats. Life has not been the same. From reading books to attending seminars, I immersed myself in PD and witnessed my life take off like I had never experienced before. I was truly beginning to discover the gift of life and the gifts in my life.

Remember how I said I thought I knew it all? I *did* until I realized that I did not know much at all. And with great gratitude for this realization, much more was to come.

If I could suggest just one thing to a new entrepreneur, it would be to start investing more into your personal growth. This might include activities that improve your awareness and identity, develop your talents and potential, or build your human capital, intellectual property, and professionalism. Such activities will enhance your quality of life, and contribute to the realization of your dreams and aspirations. Personal Development equips you with the emotional intelligence to change your life. If you think you must have money before you begin, think again! There are thousands of resources on and offline for you to begin your journey of personal growth.

Here are some great websites to get you started:

- alexechols.com
- addicted2success.com
- tinybuddha.com
- finerminds.com
- marcandangel.com

You will notice that although many people talk about the same things, people express their experiences in different manners. Still, you will begin to recognize more powerfully than ever that everyone still lives their lives and fights their own battles. This means, however, that we are able to celebrate all our joys together. Life is beautiful, and personal development amplifies our ability to empathize with others and respect their opinions.

Meditation and Stillness

I am going to tell you about one of my favorite ways to master your mindset.

Many people still attribute meditation and stillness to the Eastern World, but these practices are becoming increasingly prevalent throughout the entire world. In 2010, I rediscovered the effects of meditation while I was living in Hong Kong. That summer, my friend Mauricio and I decided to focus on "meditating, trusting the truth and accepting nature as it is."

As the weeks passed, we were accountability partners and reminded each other to remain aware of the present and the beautiful moments we were blessed to experience. The more I meditated, the more resonance I felt with the Universe.

Today, five years later, I still meditate almost every day.

Maybe sitting in complete silence is not your thing. That is okay! There are many variations of meditation and stillness available to try. Perhaps you would like to try out a guided meditation, where a spiritual teacher talks you through a few minutes of stillness. You can meditate to the soothing sounds of Tibetan bowls, hum along to sounds to clear your Chakras or even practice Vipassana by observing silence for 10+ days while meditating 10 hours each day.

You can meditate while you walk, dance, do household chores, and even cook. You can even get a meditation app on your phone that gives you meditations ranging from 2 minutes to one hour every morning. It may take a few tries to find a method that works for you. Take your time. Remember that you are learning to trust yourself and master your mind. Your efforts will pay off as you become more relaxed, soothed and present in your thoughts and actions. Meditation will increase your level of awareness, clarity, and quality of life.

Tom Cronin of the Stillness Project recounts his life as a broker in finance:

> "It was the late 80s in Australia. Greed was good. A few years in as a young broker and things started to go a little wayward for me. There was frenetic trading by day and frenetic playing by night. It took its toll and imbalances began to show. At that time I didn't know about the laws of cause and effect. I didn't know about stress management, and I certainly didn't know anything about goal setting. I was invincible, with a huge six figure salary, and we played like Masters of The Universe. But it didn't last. Cracks appeared. Insomnia, anxiety, panic attacks, then depression and eventually agoraphobia, which led to being unable to go to work.
>
> The option of doctors, psychiatrists and pharmaceuticals didn't appeal to me. I had to sort out my mind. I explored meditation and an entire cosmos of awareness opened up. The symptoms dissipated and life flourished. I continued further down that rabbit hole, exploring deeper and deeper. This took me to teacher training in India, Bali and Australia.
>
> I continued on in finance as a broker while also teaching meditation. The two worlds were extreme ends of the spectrum and yet fascinatingly were able to interplay with each other."

Imagine the benefits of sitting in silence for just a few minutes a day.

It can increase your level of awareness, it will increase your level of clarity and it will increase your quality of life. As Oprah has said, "Meditate. Breathe consciously. Listen. Pay attention. Treasure every moment and make the connection."

Trusting Yourself

As Alex has described, meditation and mindfulness will help you immensely to stay positive and calm through the trials of your entrepreneurial journey. Alongside emotional balance, self-trust is critical to healthy entrepreneurial psychology. Once you decide to start a business, you will find out very soon that you can't depend on others for encouragement. Your parents might be scared for you or try to stop you. Your friends might not take you seriously. Strangers and potential clients might mock your ideas.

You might find that nobody "gets" you.

There may be times when you feel alone. And when this happens, the only person left to trust is yourself.

This can be difficult because we are conditioned to look outside ourselves for support, security, and safety. To learn self-trust is to learn how to generate feelings of certainty when you feel insecure.

Think about this in your life. If you knew you could accomplish anything, and that no one had an agenda or opinion for or against you, how would your life be different? What would you do for a living? How much would you travel? Would you do things that you currently feel are forbidden? Chances are, nearly every aspect of your life would be radically different. By removing the restrictions of other people's expectations and judgments, you would be freer, happier, and truer to yourself.

Now is a good time to evaluate your self-trust. You can use the following checklist as a guide:

Overcoming Fear of Failure

Questions:

- When you take on a new project, do you feel (1) excited, or do you feel (2) hesitant and overly stressed?

- Are you (1) eager to seek out new experiences, or (2) do you shy away from trying new things?

- Are you generally (1) timely, or do you (2) procrastinate too much?

- Do you generally expect that things will go (1) well or (2) badly in your life? That is, when there is uncertainty surrounding an outcome in your life, what is your inner dialog?

Action Steps!

If you answered (2) to any of the above questions, then consciously or unconsciously, the fear of failure gets in the way of you taking action. Remember that the role of fear is to prevent you from doing things at which you might fail. Here are some ways to start to change that.

I. Get in touch with your emotions.

- Remove any blame and labels that you are holding onto. For instance, instead of saying, "I am so slow," you can say, "I am thorough, and I am becoming more efficient." Immediately, you look at yourself positively. Over time, you will become what you tell yourself.

- When you feel low or uncertain, acknowledge your feelings and ask yourself why. More often than not, our perceived limitations came from specific instances that caused us to develop limiting beliefs. What were these instances for you?

Write down as many that come to mind.

- Recognize that belief patterns affect your behavior and interactions, which leads to situations that reinforce your limiting beliefs. To dissolve your limiting beliefs, go through your list of situations that caused you to develop these beliefs. Imagine that these experiences belong to someone other than you. Would you develop the same conclusions about that person that you did about yourself? Chances are, you would not. See those situations objectively.

- If you do not believe that this exercise will be effective, ask yourself honestly if you have ever tried it consistently, with full intent, for an extended period of time. If not, then how do you know? You cannot know until you do it!

II. When you feel stressed, transform your physiology.

- If something stresses you out, pay attention to how you feel emotionally and physically when you think about the task at hand.

- Now, close your eyes and direct your mind to an area of your life at which you are confident and about which you feel good. Pay attention to how your body feels, particularly the tension in your muscles and the feeling in your gut. Breathe in deeply, and sit with this feeling, making a strong mental note of how it feels on every level.

- Now, direct your mind back to the area of stress, and notice how the feeling in your body changes. Did you stop breathing? Did your shoulders tense up? Do you feel weak or queasy in your gut?

- As you think about the stressful task, actively bring your body back to the state in which you felt confident. Breathe deeply, relax your muscles, and focus on your core, sending it strength. You can visualize a powerful, radiant light emanating from your core and energizing every cell in your being. Tell yourself that you are strong, capable, and confident. You are fully capable of conquering the task at hand.

III. Focus on progress, not perfection.

- Procrastination generally stems from the fear of not meeting the very high expectations that you set for yourself. But be honest with yourself: how many times has perfectionism prevented you from doing anything at all? Have goals, but realize they are something to work towards.

- Progress is what builds confidence! You gain confidence when you succeed, and more often than not, success must be earned. This does not happen without failure along the way.

- Remind yourself that most projects are not one-shot games. For instance, most companies go through multiple iterations of their websites. Every operating system builds upon the last, so nothing starts out perfect. Remember that it is okay to take your time to reach your ideal and that you do not need to be perfect now.
- In general, nobody judges you as harshly as you do. You might be investing a lot of mental energy into wondering

what people will think of you, and yet many times, they do not even care. Focus on how you feel.

- The joy of life is in experiences and changes, not in static situations. Therefore, only in your growth and improvement will you savor your journey. If something is perfect from the start, there will be no room for growth, and, therefore, there will be stagnation. You cannot find joy or fulfillment in something that is stuck. Therefore, focus on your progress and how far you have come, and this will give you momentum to reach your goal.

Overcoming Behaviors That Undermine You

Questions:

- When you see someone succeeding, especially someone close to you, do you feel (1) excited by what they have created or (2) envious? Be perfectly honest. This is a difficult question, but it is imperative that you answer honestly, without judgment.

- Are your self-care behaviors, such as diet, exercise, and sleep, (1) what you want them to be, or (2) unhealthy? Do you feel (1) in command of your life or (2) out of control? Do you eat emotionally, or are you prone to extreme behaviors to suppress how you are truly feeling?

- How is your space? Is your environment – your house, your office, or other space – (1) clean and expansive, or (2) a mess?

- When you think about a trait that you wish were different about yourself, do you (1) work to improve, or (2) feel stuck and repeat the same behaviors?

Action Steps!

This section is all about noticing how you interact with the world, and how that reflects on and influences you. Your environment is usually a direct reflection of your mental state. If you are in a state of chaos, chances are your spaces are as well. How you eat, exercise, sleep, and nurture yourself are also reflections of your mental state. If you are constantly stressed out, all of these aspects of your life inevitably take a hit. But by transforming your behaviors and environments, you can transform your mind and your productivity.

Similarly, how you feel about other people often has very little to do with them and everything to do with how you feel about yourself. If you feel envious of someone, it is not because you want to see that person fail. Rather, there is a part of you that knows you could be achieving more and doing better for yourself. So if you feel envy, it just means you need to take action!

I. Monitor your inner dialogue.

- Notice how you talk to yourself. Be aware of how you feel *about yourself* in uncomfortable situations. If you notice that it is negative, immediately reverse it.

- Be your own cheerleader. What would you like to be? How would you like to feel? Focus on this and tell yourself that every day, you are closer to those goals.

II. Question whether or not you are living up to your potential.

- Brainstorm new goals. What would make you feel awesome? Envision living your ideal life and doing amazing work. Now, from this standpoint, you will be able to appreciate the successes of others and will want to help those in need.

- Start small, but commit to your action steps. This is what will produce change. Your subconscious mind controls most of your behaviors. Therefore, you will only be able to make lasting changes by transforming your subconscious. This is a slow process, so be patient.

III. Be mindful as you eat, indulge, and interact.

- Staying calm and collected enables you to be mindful. But the reverse is true as well: when you practice mindfulness, you will find yourself feeling calmer and more empowered. These exercises are to help you to live your life from a place of feeling, a place where you are connected with yourself. Let your actions be meditative.

- When you are feeling out of control with yourself or unable to cope, you might find that you eat compulsively. If so, recognize that you have temporarily lost your power, direction, or focus. When you are eating, pay attention to your food, how you feel as you eat it, and nothing else. This will strengthen your connection with yourself and help you to live intentionally. If you have previously felt out of control around food, it will help you to get your power back.

- When you talk to someone, shut out the rest of the world and stay fully present with him or her. This will help you to stay present and will foster a better connection between you and the person with whom you are connecting.

IV. Fix your life from the outside in.

- Transform your environment so that it is expansive and inviting. You will notice an immediate improvement in your productivity and mood.

- Make good eating and regular exercise a priority. The connection between your physical health and your mood is tremendous. Make your self-care an act of love. We will talk more about this in the next chapter.

- Lastly, and most importantly, remember that changing your life for good is not about arriving at a destination and staying there. Although developing momentum is key, it is natural to fall off course from time to time, so your objective should be to improve continually, irrespective of where you find yourself.
As you become fully aware of everything you are doing and how you feel, you become more connected with yourself. You will trust yourself more, and in doing so, you will become unstoppable.

Chapter 9: Good Physical Health

"The greatest miracle on Earth is the human body. It is stronger and wiser than you may realize, and improving its ability to self-heal is within your control."
–Dr. Fabrizio Mancini

A good mindset, emotional health, and self-trust may keep you going, but a body in shape with good physical health will keep the wheels greased for you. Here's what we mean by that: as you work on getting in shape and improving your physical health, the health of your business will improve along with it.

These days, most young successful entrepreneurs also tend to be very healthy, and (let's be honest) well-toned and attractive!

Why is that?

Good Physical Health

As a generation, young people are taking better care of themselves by exercising regularly, eating healthfully, meditating, investing in personal growth, believing in themselves, and connecting with other like-minded, empowered individuals.

The more health-conscious you are, the happier, healthier, and fitter you will be. In doing so, you will attract a higher caliber tribe.

It is important to remember that how you do anything is how you do everything. This is a key element of success as an entrepreneur. In this chapter, we will talk more about how that works.

Taking Full Control

You want to run a successful business. Would you not also want to be successful in all the areas of your life? Of course! You are here to take full control of all of these areas.

In the previous chapters, we spoke about overcoming depression, establishing self-trust, and taking control of your mental and emotional states. Now I will talk about taking control of your physical health by sharing my own experiences.

Jack Delosa of The Entourage once said, "One of the things I often think about is that nothing is easy and therefore if something is easy, it is often nothing."

The Two-Week Notice

Maintaining a healthy, balanced life is not always easy, but it is one of the most important things for you to stay on top of your entrepreneurial game.

Growing up, I was a pretty heavy kid. Who am I fooling? At 5'4" and 230+ pounds, I was damn near obese. People called me Fat Albert or the Kool-Aid Man, which I eventually got used to, but when one of my father's coworkers called me a sumo wrestler, I decided to change things for myself. But between my early teens and mid-twenties, my weight yo-yoed up and down a lot.

On the one hand, I wanted to be more attractive to women and not to be made fun of. On the other hand, I always felt like I did not have time to go to the gym after working a full-time job, which was generally to be followed by dinner and drinks with friends.

Here was my reality check: not having time is a big fat excuse (pun intended). The way my priorities were then, I did not give my physical health the respect it deserved. So I scaled back on the frequent dinners out and started hitting the gym.

Amazingly, as I got into better physical shape, every aspect of my life and work improved dramatically. To lose the weight, I focused on improving not only my eating and fitness habits, but my attitude towards them. Being in a space of peak performance, physically, I noticed an increase in my confidence at networking events and during sales calls. It boosted my desire to become a greater man and leader.

Good Physical Health

Hitting personal fitness records in sprints, pull-ups and push-ups also allowed me to hit personal records within my businesses. Month over month, I would make double or triple the amount of revenue I had made the previous month. At one point, I generated what I had normally made in one payment period in a single day. In spite of that, I still found the time to train at my boxing gym and take a Tango lesson. I do not say any of this to impress you, but to solidify the idea that 'health is true wealth.'

In reality, I was never too busy to do any of those things before. I had just chosen to believe that I was.

Fitness

If you feel *too busy*, start small. Go for a 15-minute brisk walk or run to increase the blood circulation throughout your body. Get a higher desk so you can stand up a bit more during the workday. Maybe do a half-hour of yoga, which reduces stress and burns fat. Good physical health keeps you alert and keeps your mind moving forward. Any personal trainer would suggest that you engage in moderate to high-intensity workouts at least a few times a week while still doing some exercise each day.

Physical activity is not difficult to incorporate. Find something you enjoy. Whether you go to the gym, take a dance class, or sign up for your community softball league, it is important to stay healthy and active and to also understand that the bodies and minds we have today are our greatest assets. 'The more we take care of them, the more they will take care of us over time.

Sleep

I confess that I cannot function with accuracy and speed without at least 7.5 hours of sleep.

Being sufficiently rested is important for both short and long-term success. As an entrepreneur, you are most creative when your brain is operating in a peak state. We are often told to neglect sleep, but this always takes a toll on your mood, productivity, and accuracy. Even though sleeping more means fewer hours to hustle, the quality of your work and experiences will improve dramatically.

More importantly, you will artificially shorten your life – and the amount you can accomplish – if you routinely deprive your body of sleep. Your cognition, alertness, and reaction times are directly influenced by how rested you are.

Everyone requires a slightly different amount of sleep to function optimally. But here are some tips to help you to maximize both the duration and quality of your sleep:

Good Physical Health

- Cut out non-essential items on your to-do list.

- Find out when you are most productive and creative. If you are a night owl (as many creative people are), be disciplined and firm about when you need to go to bed and wake up. Do not feel pressured to change your schedule to match everyone else's.

- Exercise during the day so that your body goes into a deeper state of sleep for longer. Get as tired as you can by the time you hit the sack.

- Avoid stimulating foods such as chocolate and coffee before bed. These foods can prevent you from getting the sleep you need.

- Avoid eating heavy foods, especially closer to bedtime. Your body will have to work overtime to process it as you sleep.

- Always go to sleep inspired. I like to listen to binaural music when I sleep to deepen my state.

- As far as possible, try to stick to a regular sleep schedule.

Dietary Lifestyle

Food is the most important factor when it comes to your health. Living off of Ramen Noodles is unsustainable and will harm you greatly in the long run. While this subject is vast and well beyond the scope of this book, here are some tips to get you started.

- You can usually find heavily discounted produce at your local supermarket so that if you are on a budget, you can nourish yourself inexpensively.

- Prepare foods in advance and have them in the refrigerator or freezer for ready use. This will also help you to reduce your spending on eating out.

- Minimize processed foods, which can rob you of massive amounts of energy. The average person on a standard American diet expends 70% of his or her energy on digestion.

- Fresh vegetable juice is the best energy drink there is. There are many inexpensive centrifugal juicers. A simple, fast, inexpensive juice might be something with carrots and celery.

Recreation

All work and no play will make you boring and miserable. It also puts you at risk of reaching a point when your brain and body refuse to work altogether. When you prioritize your hobbies, you will automatically find that you are more motivated and productive.

Here are some steps to help you:

Good Physical Health

- Set milestones for your work, both big and small, and reward yourself when you meet them by engaging in your chosen recreational activities.

- Find activities that expand you. Try new things that require skills that you have never tried out to keep you stimulated, creative, and spontaneous.

- You can use your recreation time to meet new people or connect with people who you want to know better. This is a great way to build your network in a way that is authentic and fun.

- Travel is a fantastic way to stay inspired. Find ways to conduct your business remotely so that you have the ability to experience the world while running your business.

Section III

Connecting the Entrepreneur

Chapter 10: Connecting More Authentically

"If you spent 100 percent of your waking hours thinking about how you can help absolutely everyone you come in contact with, you will find everything else tends to take care of itself. The world will suddenly be in your corner."
–Scott Dinsmore

Let me paint a picture for you:

Steve is a young entrepreneur who is just starting to work for himself. He and two of his closest friends (also entrepreneurs) are invited to their first exclusive Entrepreneurs Networking Event where 50 professionals have been personally selected to attend. Steve is pretty excited!

After Steve is clean-cut and ready, the three of them head to the event feeling increasingly excited about how many business cards they can snag. They are so excited that they decide to make it a competition.

They walk in and survey the room. There is a fountain of chocolate fondue on the left and a champagne pyramid on the right. And all around them are dozens of young people enthralled in conversation with each other over hors d'oeuvres and bubbly. The three friends grab a few glasses each and decide to split up – game on.

Steve is pumped up to start attracting a lot of people. He sees a pair of individuals laughing and walks over to them. Their names are Sean and Jamie. They are talking about some of their best memories studying abroad in Spain.

Steve interjects without hesitation, shakes Sean and Jamie's hands and says, "Hi, I'm Steve. Nice to meet you both! What do you do?"

Sean and Jamie quickly respond that they work in finance and entertainment, respectively, and continue their conversation with each other.

Steve is confused. Were they uninterested in knowing what he did as a profession? Did they not have the courtesy to ask him about his business in return? Were they just plain rude?

Nevertheless, he decides to try to integrate into the next fun-looking group. Maybe the first one was just a fluke.

This group is made up of two girls, both named Ashley, and a guy named Scott. Steve waits for his cue before introducing himself to the three. "Hi, I am Steve. How are you guys doing tonight?"

Both girls say, "Nice to meet you too, are you enjoying yourself?" Scott responds, "Doing well man, it's a lot of cool people here to meet." Steve then says, "Yes, I agree! So what do you guys do?"

The three of them give their answers, continue talking to Steve for a minute or two more, and eventually return to their previous conversation. Steve is left wondering, "What the hell is going on tonight?!"

So what exactly is going on? In both conversations, why did the two groups continue their conversations without Steve? Did his breath stink? Had he spilled chocolate fondue on his tie?

None of the above.

Steve's issue was a condition called the "I Just Want to Know What You Do' syndrome. As you saw, Steve's first or second question to both groups was "so, what do you do?" Many young (and older) professionals suffer from this condition when introducing themselves to others in a networking or professional environment.

The problem with this question is that the recipients have no way of knowing if you are asking because:

1. You want to know so you can help them,
2. You want to know so you can get THEM to help YOU, or
3. You just do not have any better questions to ask

Only one of those is worth their effort to respond to, and the other two are so self-centered that taking a one in three chance is often not worth it.

Initially, both girls were interested in Steve, and Scott was friendly with him. But when all he wanted to talk about was what they did, they ignored him.

Here is a wake-up call for Steve (and maybe for you, too!): if you want to be a successful entrepreneur, then you must start asking better questions than "what do you do?" when you meet people. This is especially true at networking events.

So how can an entrepreneur like you avoid being scrutinized and become an outcast like Steve during your next networking event?

Learn to BAMF: *Be Authentic More, Friend.*

Authenticity, according to many dictionaries, means "genuine and undisputed in origin." In a personal development context, authenticity means being your purest, truest and most genuine self.

In networking, authenticity manifests itself in making genuine connections with others.

Connecting More Authentically

It sounds relatively simple, but like a muscle, it is something that needs to be built up with practice over time. Here are two simple tips you can use to practice connecting authentically.

1. Find Connection Points

The need to connect starts from birth. We are conditioned at such a young age to look for connection points to interact with and be accepted by others.

Connection points are exactly what they sound like: talking points or common experiences over which you and another person can form a connection. Successful connection points can be as simple as two individuals loving sushi or the same basketball team or the same brand of sportswear. By finding the points of connection, you start to build a bridge between you and them.

Remember Sean and Jamie? What Steve did not know was that those two people had only met each other a few minutes before. Yet because they immediately found a connection point around their experiences studying abroad in Spain, by the time Steve got to them they were chatting and laughing like old friends.

Steve failed to look for any connection points and went straight to asking "what do you do?" Contrary to his expectations, this tactic left him stranded and confused.

2. Ask Better Questions

One of the most important habits of being a successful entrepreneur is being able to ask well-defined and thoughtful questions. By asking better questions, we not only present ourselves as being educated and articulate, but we can also determine the energies and personalities with whom we are most compatible.

Where Steve did not succeed in this context was in his abrupt and direct approach. Instead of asking "what do you do," he could have asked more creative questions such as:

- "What are some of your favorite projects?"
- "What are you most passionate about?"
- "What is the most exciting thing going on in your life right now?"
- "What is your 'Why' in life?"

The answers to these questions would probably have included something about what these people did for their jobs, would have also started much more stimulating conversations and possibly laid the foundation for a great professional relationship. Such questions can create a dialog that transcends mere work and delves into purpose, ambition, passion and excitement.

By finding connection points and asking more thoughtful questions, you allow yourself and others to step outside of the professional box. Instead of talking about work (the expected and boring topic at networking events), you can have a dialog that transcends mere work into purpose, ambition, passion and excitement. By going outside the professional world, you invite others to be more engaging and fun in their responses.

In our previous example, Steve had not even made it this far, but now that we have gone over some tips, let's imagine Steve's interaction in an updated, more authentic fashion.

Steve walks up to Sean and Jamie, smiles, and listens to their conversation for a moment. Realizing they are talking about Spain (a country he has also visited), he enters the conversation with "Spain is an awesome place! I absolutely loved the time I spent there as well. Did either one of you happen to attend La Tomatina while you were there?"

"No" Sean and Jamie reply, "but that sounds fun, what is it?"

Steve has successfully found a connection point. The ensuing conversation lasts several minutes and includes lots of laughter as the three share stories of their fun times in Spain.

Partway through the conversation, once they have spoken quite a bit about Spain, Steve decides to ask Jamie and Sean, "so what are two of your favorite projects or endeavors you are currently involved with?" Both other people are very excited to answer that question, as it gives them a chance to talk about their passion projects. By the time the three are done talking about this topic, the conversation has lasted over half an hour. They have not only figured out some great ways to help each other succeed, but are also becoming good friends.

Things changed for Steve once he changed his approach. He is now on his way to becoming a master connector.

Now, not every networking story is going to turn out like Steve's. Even with practice, finding connection points and asking thoughtful questions, not everyone is going to want to talk to you or form a strong connection with you. And that is okay. Mastering these techniques will make the connections that do form strong, meaningful and supportive enough that the ones that do not work out will not even matter to you.

So be like Steve. Go forth and BAMF.

Chapter 11: Outgrowing and Elevating Your Network

*"Lower your expectations of what you think life owes you
& raise your standards on what you give to life."*
–Jairek Robbins

What they say is true: "the higher your aspirations, the more friends you may end up losing." But this has a beautiful silver lining: you will end up with the tribe you are meant to be with.

Perhaps it is a tribe of all-stars. You just need the courage to take the less-traveled road.

Growing up on the South Side of Chicago, I was destined to do one of two things:

1. Remain in the hood with hopes of one day making it out

The Two-Week Notice

2. Excel in school and be a leader in my community to gain more opportunities

At a young age, the latter would require that I start accepting the fact that I would outgrow old friends simply due to circumstances. But I still had no idea just how blank my canvas would be as I grew older.

You can spot the dip in my transition here: my Catholic grade school consisted of 95%+ African Americans, my Catholic high school consisted of about 30% African Americans, and then I was off to one of the best colleges in the United States.

There, African Americans were a whopping 8% of the student body. And now I am in Sydney, Australia for a few months each year, and the numbers are even lower.

Throughout this transition, I have noticed fewer and fewer of my fellow black people surround me, especially men. Throughout most of my past, I was the only African American in most of my enrichment programs, networks, and international study abroad groups.

And, to be honest, it was (and still is) quite disheartening.

With Simon Sinek's book *Start with Why*, you will find that it is necessary to know *why* you are doing something.

Back then, I was asking the wrong 'why.' My questions consisted more of 'Why me? Why am I being blessed with all of these wonderful opportunities when so many people are struggling?" It was such a consistent message in my mind, as I looked around wondering and wishing to have more of my people surrounding me. And one day, it started to click and make a bit more sense to me: simply because my brothers and sisters are not here with me right now does not mean that they never will be. And if my brothers are falling, I will fly – to lift them up.

Similar to Sinek, who talks about a shift in perspective, my friend Jairek has shared his two principles on how to view things differently, and turn the ordinary into extraordinary in our everyday lives.

His two principles are:

- The ability to shift our perception of how we view a specific activity
- The ability to shift our procedure as to how we go about physically doing the activity

Within these two principles, Jairek once asked me, "If you had the ability to take something and shift your perception on it...what freedom do you feel that will provide for you in your life and business? How much more effective will you be? How would it affect your personal life?"

Suddenly, my *Why* had changed from a question to a statement. My 'why' was now elevated, and my life's purpose became more apparent and I started to look at everyone around me, regardless of color and background, as my *people*.

The Two-Week Notice

Note: even as I write this today on March 18th, I realize just how important it is to find your 'why' and use it as a GPS to reach your goal, and continue to repeat the process.

To give you some examples, here are a few of my current *why's*:

1. Retire my mother and father
2. Travel internationally with my sister and friends
3. Inspire and empower others to growth & greatness

It is so important to find your 'why'. Use it as a GPS to reach your goal, and continue to repeat the process.

Chapter 12: Finding a Mentor

Stepping into your greatness can seem daunting. Not only are you exploring your new path alone and searching for others like you as you go, but you do not even know which way to go yet. You are exploring alien terrain.

Or are you?

I bet you can think of a few people who have already made the leap you are making. Maybe they even did it in the same industry as you.

These people will be your mentors.

Starting today, the most important thing you can do is to find a mentor. Think of Yoda from *Star Wars*, Dumbledore from *Harry Potter*, or Gandalf from *Lord of the Rings*. A mentor is somebody who can guide you from where you are to where you want to be. He or she has the knowledge, wisdom and experience to help you discover your unlimited potential. Often, a mentor has already accomplished what you are setting out to achieve.

My mentor has helped me with the following:

- A job as a contributing author at ASPIRE Magazine
- Introductions to organizations that qualify for GameChangers 500
- Acceptance to Awesomeness Fest
- Group masterminds in Costa Rica, Las Vegas, and San Diego
- Connections and friendships with world class entrepreneurs

It is imperative to create a mutually beneficial relationship. In my experience, there are plenty of people who will give you advice from time to time out of the goodness of their hearts. This is fantastic, and I would take these individuals up on the offer to soak in their wisdom. However, there are benefits to offering something in return so you can move from being a mentee to a business partner.

How do you do this?

For starters, let's identify who your ideal mentor right now is. In this example, we are going to use the stereotypical CEO in corporate America.

He is wildly successful monetarily, and you may not be capable of making him more money. However, he is most likely stressed out, unhealthy, and has strained relationships with his family because of his work hours. Can you think of a way to help this overly stressed businessman?

As stated in Chapter 2, Tony Robbins, who was voted by Accenture as one of the Top 50 Business Intellectuals in the World, states that we have six needs as human beings:

1. Certainty - Assurance you can avoid pain and gain pleasure.

2. Uncertainty - The need for variety, the unknown, change, new stimuli.

3. Significance - Feeling unique, important, special or needed.

4. Love/Connection - A strong feeling of closeness or union with someone or something.

5. Growth - An expansion of capacity, capability or understanding.

6. Contribution - A sense of service and focus on helping, giving to and supporting others.

After reflecting on your unique genius, how can you use your unique skill set to aid this stressed out businessman? Perhaps you have been practicing yoga for the last couple of years, and you recognize its ability to relax, restore, and transform people. Maybe you can form a mutually beneficial relationship with that CEO by sharing your passion of yoga to help him get healthy and decrease his stress while he helps advance your career.

From there, you need to find a way to approach that individual. The easiest way to do this is by tapping into your network. In an ideal world, you have been building up your LinkedIn profile, have tons of influential Facebook friends and have dozens of email addresses that you have accumulated over the years. From there, you can look through your connections to find one that may be able to offer you introductions to that person.

The best way to discover this is by using LinkedIn. Search for the individual that you would love to get in contact with and see who in your network is connected with that person on LinkedIn. If you do have any connections, ask your contact to make an introduction.

If you would like to take a more direct approach, you can consider contacting your potential mentors directly via email or LinkedIn. When doing this, do not immediately start pitching yourself. Do some research on these individuals so you can create custom emails explaining how much you admire them for ____ (insert your own idea) and ask whether you can speak with them for 15 minutes about how they did ____ (insert your own idea).

This direct approach worked for me while on my journey of finding my Yoda. I first heard Andrew Hewitt, Founder of GameChangers 500, speak the summer after my senior year of college. His story of pursuing his purpose resonated with every fiber of my being. After hearing him speak, I

Finding a Mentor

knew that I needed to find a way to get to know him better and learn from him.

After sending him emails for two months, we finally arranged a phone call, and he agreed be my mentor. Within a short time, he helped me land a job in my dream industry.

I was beyond ecstatic to start this new journey, but I also wanted my relationship with Andrew to continue. I had learned so much from him in under four months, and I knew that there was still so much more to explore. So I spent a lot of time reflecting on how I, a broke twenty-two-year-old with no work experience, could provide something of value to a best-selling author, speaker, and entrepreneur.

After evaluating my strengths further, I realized that a passion of mine was online marketing. I also noticed that Andrew's company, GameChangers 500, was not using social media to effectively communicate with its online audience.

Eureka!

I made a pitch to Andrew to allow me to manage his startup's online community for free, and in return he would continue being my mentor.

This way, I could develop a case study for my paying clients in the future.

The Two-Week Notice

As a result of looking for more ways to help Andrew's organization succeed, this mutually beneficial partnership blossomed into more than I ever could have imagined.

To find your mentor, start by answering some of the following questions:

- Who do I know that is doing what I am doing but is five or ten years ahead of me?
- What don't I know about my business, and who can I approach to help me learn it?
- Who inspires me?
- Whose work makes my jaw drop?
- If I can't approach those people, who might be just as good?
- Who in my industry is known for being a good/supportive/enthusiastic mentor?
- What are the 3-5 goals I have for working with a mentor?
- What kind of communication style do I like?
- How do I respond to constructive criticism?
- How will I know when a mentorship has lasted long enough?

It is important to start answering these questions so you can begin the process of understanding who you are and what you represent. In turn, when you realize whom you want to reach out to, you will have an actionable plan.

Section IV

Growing the Entrepreneur

Chapter 13: Building Collaborations and Partnerships

"You can build the most beautiful place in the world but it takes people." –Walt Disney

By now, you should be starting to feel ready to roar as an entrepreneur and make your voice heard all throughout the real world.

You have learned about making authentic connections, responding to outgrowing your network, and finding a mentor to help you get started.

To finish up this section on authentic entrepreneurial connection, we are going to look at another great way to increase your chances of becoming successful: joint ventures, collaborations and partnerships.

Most "regular" jobs require you at some point to form a team. Entrepreneurship does not require this, but collaborations can be very helpful and important to gain exposure, make connections, and develop your business. Partnerships open you up to fresh ideas, varied perspectives, massively expanded skill sets, and much higher bandwidth. You can discover synergies that enable you to create projects that would be impossible on your own.

What Does a Partnership Look Like?

One of the joys of entrepreneurship is the feeling of controlling your destiny. You are the visionary of your organization, so you can finally ditch some of the negative programming you learned from prior work experiences.

You do not have to think of business as an 'I win and you lose' type situation. Instead, you can begin to view business as a way to collaborate with other people who believe what you believe.

During the first year of operation, No Typical Moments had an extremely niche service offering: social media marketing. There were numerous positives and negatives to this scope of services. On the one hand, if your service offering is very specific, people will consider you to be an expert. This means that you may have an easier time winning contracts because you won't come across as a "we do anything and everything" type of small business.

On the other hand, sometimes clients need more than just your niche offering. They may need SEO, blog writing or email marketing, to name a few. This is where partnerships can come into play.

If you find the right partners who offer complementary services, you can package your offerings together and create an even better opportunity for a lead. For example, No Typical Moments combined our services with Social Diva Media to work with a gospel group for their appearance on the Oprah Winfrey Network. No Typical Moments handled the Twitter strategy while Social Diva Media acted as the project managers. None of this would have been possible if we stayed with the mentality that other businesses were competitors to be vanquished.

So Partnerships Are Awesome, Right?

Well, they can be. They certainly were for Andrew in his first year with No Typical Moments, and it has worked pretty well for the three of us in writing this book.

But please understand this: rushing into a partnership just for the sake of having one probably will not help you.

Forming a partnership with anyone and everyone to get ahead quickly is a lot like asking everyone "what do you do?" at a networking event. Chances are the other parties will see through to your self-centered motives and decline to work with you—or else they will use your services for free and move on.

Building Collaborations and Partnerships

Furthermore, partnerships can sometimes create as many issues as they solve.

Have you ever had to work on a team where another team member came up with a truly terrible idea and would not let it go? Or did mediocre or shoddy work that you then had to re-do? Professional partnerships can easily run into those problems – except now your paycheck and your professional reputation are at their mercy.

This is why choosing your potential partners very, *very* carefully is imperative. It is also why partnering with friends just because they are your friends is not always a good idea – if the partnership collapses, it could destroy the friendship along with it.

Also, understand that collaborations cannot replace the effort that you put into your brand and business. Even if you are looking to leverage another business' success to catapult your own, you must always maintain your brand's strength and focus alongside your collaboration. Look at it as something you are doing on top of your regular business work, not instead of it.

Finally, here are several other tips to keep in mind when considering partnerships:

- People can break their word. Be extremely careful whom you trust. Make sure you write a contract for any agreement.

- You will most likely have to reconcile your personal freedom or goals with the other person's objectives in some way. Be prepared to compromise.

- You might be able to push yourself farther alone. On your own, you will have more fuel, more freedom, and more responsibility. This might land you farther than someone else's help.

- If you have too much of a security net, you might never take action. So before you enter a partnership, ask yourself very honestly if you are doing so purely as a way to stay safe. If so, you are sabotaging your success by not trusting yourself and taking action.

- Your time is limited. Be sure to prioritize. If your time and effort are being invested into a partnership, it will come at the expense of personal projects.

Preparing to Find Good Partners

Networking is critical to finding good partners. But before you go charging out to network with everyone you can,

Building Collaborations and Partnerships

make sure you are prepared and have a strategy. Here are a few tips to prepare for networking with potential partners:

1. Know what you want to accomplish with a partnership and have a crystal clear vision for these goals. One helpful way to do this is to write down your mission or primary goals, then write out 4-6 projects related to that mission or those goals where you feel you could use support or help from a partner.

2. Think about people who are already established in a similar or complementary field whom you feel can help you achieve those goals. Also consider those people you truly admire and want to support. Feel free to chat with fellow entrepreneurs for inspiration—they may know people who would be perfect for you to partner with!

3. Research their fields and the areas their business can improve.

4. Now forget about what you need for a while, and brainstorm creative ways in which you can help these people to achieve *their* goals. Know your strengths and look for ways to use those strengths to help them build their businesses.

5. Write a short and compelling document summarizing items 3 and 4 for each potential partner, which you can present to and discuss with them at your first meeting. You already know what you want from them.

Leave that out of it for now. Your primary focus is on letting them know how the partnership will help and serve them.

Connecting with Potential Partners

As you brainstorm these possible partners, it may help you to sort them into three categories:

- **Easy Connections** (these are people you know or can easily get an introduction to)

- **Stretch Prospects** (these are people you do not know, but may be in the network of someone you know – or someone *they* know)

- **Long Shots** (these are high-profile people you have no apparent connection to outside of maybe following them on social media or subscribing to their email list)

Building Collaborations and Partnerships

Once you have sorted them this way, you will have two potential ways to prioritize who you research and prepare to approach: either you can start with easy connections and work your way up, or you can start with the long shots and work your way down.

The first option will be the simplest and most likely to find you a partner, but may insulate you from higher-profile candidates. The second will be much higher-risk and will require more legwork, but could pay off by putting a much bigger and stronger partner in your corner. Whichever method you choose, pick 4-6 names and start researching them by the process above.

Next, facilitate an introduction to each potential partner that you do not already know (a cold email will not work for you in this context). There are two great ways to do this:

Ask a friend who knows them to introduce you over email (or in person, if feasible).

Go to a conference or event where they are speaking, meet them there, and instead of being like the other autograph-seekers, tell them very briefly your best idea of how you can help them and ask to discuss it with them later. This differentiation, making it about them rather than about you, may get their attention enough to set up a meeting or phone call.

Once the intro has been made, here is a template you could use to reach out to or follow up with that person:

The Two-Week Notice

Dear _____,

I wanted to reach out to you personally to follow up with you after our introduction. I admire your work for (authentic reason) and I believe I can help make your _____ even better.

Here are a few ideas:
(BRIEF bulleted list describing your best ideas)

If you are interested, I am happy to discuss these further with you. Please let me know and we can set up a call at your convenience.

Best,
(Your Name)

Then set up your meeting or call and tell them about your ideas. Remember, your primary goal is to show how helping them with their projects actually helps and serves them and their goals.

Working In a Partnership

We understand that you are a hungry, ambitious entrepreneur, and you want to get started in your first partnership ASAP. But do not go so fast that you try to make things work where there's not a good fit. The good news is, a more experienced entrepreneur will likely see if something is not working way before you do since they have been through many similar situations before. They will likely see potential issues in the very first pitch meet-

Building Collaborations and Partnerships

ing, and tell you yes or no up front based on those issues. Many of them will say no. That's okay. As you learn and practice active and persistent patience, you will be able to thank them sincerely and move on to the next prospect.

But when one does say yes, and you start to create and build the partnership, keep these three questions in mind:

1. Can our business model make money?
2. Are we working equally as partners?
3. Am I happy?

You might find yourself going through a few projects before you find one that fits, and that is okay. Do not be too quick to give up on something because it becomes a bit difficult, but if you find yourself answering "no" to those questions frequently, do not be afraid to walk away either.

You might find the right partnership after the first try or the fifteenth. But always continue to build something based on your mission and continue to help others and change the world. As the time passes, and you develop your business and brand, you will go from being the 'featured as' joint partner to the "sponsored by" joint partner.

Chapter 14: Build Your Brand

"Great stories happen to those who can tell them. The future of branding is marketing with people, not at them."
–John Morgan

Think Richard Branson of Virgin. Think Steve Jobs of Apple. Think Michael Jordan of the NBA. What do they all have in common besides their great legacies?

Brands.

They found what they were good at, whether it was creating products, delivering services, or playing a sport, and created prominent brands around those skills. No one ever thinks of Virgin without Richard Branson entering the conversation and the same goes for Jordan and Jobs.

We like Seth Godin's definition of a brand: "a set of associated expectations, memories, stories, and relationships."

But not all brands have to be globally renown to be successful and effective. Lisa Messenger, the Owner and Creative Director of The Messenger Group, publishes the monthly magazine *Collective* which has beautifully branded itself as a thoughtful magazine for the entrepreneurs, game changers, rule breakers, thought leaders and creative minds of the world.

Lisa's aim with The Collective is to "inform and inspire a community of proactive and engaged thinkers who want to make an impact on the world." With monthly highlights focusing on the technology, style, travel and the lifestyle of an entrepreneur, The Messenger Group is leading the way with its brand.

So what is your story? Where are you exceptional? What are some of your greatest interests? Get out a pen and pad and begin to write down your answers to these questions.

What is your story? What, as an entrepreneur, do you feel you would like to share with the world? Is it within finances, health or cuisine? Or does it deal with traveling? It can be anything you enjoy – you will just need to be able to create your story around it. This will be the foundation of your brand. These days, companies do not engage very well with clients unless they have proper branding, and thus they lose the ability to build powerful, engaged communities of raving fans.

So How Will You Build Your Brand?

It is important to consider whether you want to build online, offline or both. In today's world of social media, many people are opting to do both by using traditional means of networking at events and mailing physical ads while also sending promotions via social media channels such as Facebook and Google. This allows for intimate connections and breakthroughs while still having the reach and leverage to connect with individuals from the other side of the world.

So which do you choose? With the pen and pad that is in front of you right now, whether you would like your business to be brick and mortar, virtual or a hybrid. Nothing is ever set in stone, but it is essential to have a roadmap. When starting out as an entrepreneur, do not be afraid to become your own best fan, spokesperson and sales force. You are the walking representation of your brand. Embrace that, especially if you are looking to start out as lean as possible!

Unless you have a family member or friend that can help you with all the initial resources, you must work your tail off to gain exposure for your brand. Hustle until doing so becomes a passion and turns into a natural part of your business and life.

Remember: consistency is key.

Go build that brand.

Chapter 15: Find Your Tribe

"A tribe is a group of people connected to one another, connected to a leader, and connected to an idea. For millions of years, human beings have been part of one tribe or another. A group needs only two things to be a tribe: a shared interest and a way to communicate." –Seth Godin

Most small children choose their friends based on availability (and the presence or absence of cooties). Adolescents generally pick friends based on similar interests or how cool people think they are. But rarely do people consciously choose their companions based on the effects those people will have on them. As an entrepreneur, this is exactly what you need to do. As you are going out in the world building your business and brand, your circle of friends is more important than ever.

Some may refer to this circle of friends as their *posse*. Others may still use the traditional term, *network*. We like to refer to a band of like-minded souls as a *tribe*.

Although the idea of a network generally connotes a professional group of individuals working in the same or similar fields, the modern-day meaning of *tribe* defines that same group of individuals as being linked by cultural, goal-oriented or social ties. Members of a tribe can be from all walks of life, coming together to help each other reach goals and stay motivated.

Over the last few years, the three of us have worked on projects with some incredible, like-minded people. We have grown and flourished because we have continued to surround ourselves with so many wise, experienced people. They supported us and their goals resonated with our own.

It is said that it takes a village to raise a child, but it takes a tribe to develop him or her to be the best version of him or herself.

How We Found Our Tribes

You might remember from the introduction of this book that the three of us met at a conference called Awesomeness Fest. Awesomeness Fest (or A-Fest for short) is a tribe-forming conference and an extraordinary personal development experience.

This is an important point. The A-Fest tribe that we three decided to join had two parts. First, there were the people who hosted and presented at the event: people like Khailee Ng (Venture Partner for 500 Startups), Joel Neoh (Founder of Groupon Malaysia), and Vishen Lakhiani (CEO and Founder of Mindvalley). These were entrepreneurs we all looked up to and could not wait to learn from. We were joining a tribe that they had come to Bali to join and inspire.

And then there were the 250 other people in attendance from all walks of life who all believed what we believe. Each one of us was called to this event for a very specific reason – to realize and understand that we are not alone in our quests for pursuing our dreams. Together, we can achieve remarkable things to make the world a better place.

Clearly we could not meet *everyone* there (though some of us tried), but as we were all open to being part of this big tribe, we met some pretty cool new friends: each other. This book is a direct result of our finding and joining a tribe together.

What Will Your Tribe Be Like?

Your tribe consists of the people that resonate with the ideal version of yourself. So as you start looking for your tribe, think about the kind of person you want to be. Imagine: what do you look like when you are at your best physically, intellectually, in your job, and in your personal life? What kind of demeanor do you have? Most importantly, how do you want to feel? Whom do you admire?

Your tribe members are people who will help you to realize your ideal version of yourself because they are also doing amazing things, are working to become their ideal selves and are living their ideal lives as well. They believe in and pursue their own dreams, and when they recognize the same spark in you, they naturally believe in and support yours as well.

As long as you are willing to put in just as much as you are looking to get out of it, your tribe will lift you up professionally and personally. Your business will grow, and your network will expand. You won't just go to places like A-Fest, TEDx events, Burning Man, SXSW—you will start creating them with your tribe. With your tribe around you, you will do things you never imagined.

How Do I Find My Tribe?

According to Jim Rohn, you are the average of the five people with whom you spend the most time. Think about those five people in your life. Are they positive? Do they keep good care of their bodies? What type of jobs do they have? Are they in healthy relationships? Now, imagine if those five people were all striving to be the healthiest and happiest versions of themselves. What type of impact would that make in your life? Think of the limitless possibilities if you surrounded yourself with people who would not let you fail!

I am the first person to admit that finding my tribe was one of the most difficult things I have done since graduating from university. While I partied hard in college, I no longer saw this as a viable form of long-term happiness.

Find Your Tribe

But then, where does a 22-year-old find other young people if not at the bar?

I struggled with this question for a very long time and became the most anti-social I had been in my entire life. For over a year, my nights were spent at home watching reruns of The Big Bang Theory on TBS. This was not the ideal way to find a social crowd by any stretch of the imagination, but I felt like I needed this break from the bar life so I could reevaluate what I truly wanted out of friendship.

What I found was that I was not just looking for a few good laughs over beer. I wanted soulful connections with other human beings in which I could talk about my deepest desires and dreams, while at the same time, be able to dance the night away while listening to idiotic music.

I felt displaced for a very long time while starting my organization, as if I did not belong in society. As things continued to progress and grow, I did not know whether people actually liked me. If my company fell apart, would they still look at me the same way or shun me as if I was an outcast from society?

This messed with my head, which is why I found it hard to interact with somebody outside of the entrepreneurial community. I felt that other entrepreneurs could share my pain and were dealing with similar types of issues that society at large would never understand. But I also preferred to stop hanging out with entrepreneurs because the only thing we would talk about was business.

I wanted something more, and I was at a loss for words to articulate it.

This process was difficult but completely worth it. Because right at that low point where I could not figure out exactly what I wanted or how to get it, I found Awesomeness Fest and with it, my tribe. This was where Alex, Sulinya and I met.

What I learned from the experience at Awesomeness Fest was that I am not alone in the conquest of pursuing my deepest desires. In fact, I found 250 other people who all believed what I believe. We were all called to this event for a very specific reason – to realize and understand that we are not alone in the conquest of pursuing our dreams. When I grasped this concept, I realized that No Typical Moments represented possibility and hope to make the world a better place. And by not stepping into my greatness and seeing how far I could take it, that I would be doing a disservice to everybody wanting to align with the organization.

Since this realization, I have:

- Worked with the first personal development company to have an IPO
- Hired over half a dozen pro-bono volunteers
- Matched year one's total revenue within the first two months of year two
- Been featured in GOOD Magazine and Triple Pundit
- Worked with the 2014 Pittsburgh Marathon

Find Your Tribe

This potential to create a movement was inside of myself all along even if I did not believe it. When you speak your truth and pursue something bigger than yourself, people will listen and gravitate towards your cause. However, it can only start when you, the founder, believe it from within.

Wait, Do I *Have* To Go To A-Fest?

No, you do not *have* to go to A-Fest. You do not have to go to Burning Man or SXSW or World Domination Summit either. You certainly can if you want (and you will have a blast if you do), but you can find your tribe without shelling out money for a conference pass and a plane ticket halfway around the world.

There are hundreds of other groups, activities, masterminds and clubs you can look into to help you find a tribe. Start talking to others and begin searching the web for tribes with which you can get involved today. Look for people who share interests with you, who work in your industry, or who have similar values. Ask them who their tribes are and how they got together. (Maybe you already know some of those people from your authentic networking!) We guarantee that you will create some of the best experiences with some of the best people once you find your tribe.

Chapter 16: Finding Joy in the Entrepreneurial Journey

"'Entrepreneur' just denotes that you recognize that you're doing things across disciplines and that you're blazing your own path." –Pharrell Williams

We have to be insanely passionate about the business to persuade others to work with us. However, we cannot allow our happiness to depend on success or failure of the company. In fact, our happiness must precede success.

Nearly all entrepreneurs will admit that the journey of entrepreneurship is not easy. At times, it can be much more difficult than working for someone else, especially in the start-up phase. But you have chosen this journey because you have realized the normal working world is not for you. You do not mind putting in extra hours to obtain results, and you want to go out into the world and share your gifts.

Finding Joy in the Entrepreneurial Journey

In this book, we have shared some of our most thoughtful, vulnerable and truthful stories from our respective journeys to aid you in your journey: from transitioning out of the traditional workplace, to learning how to connect more authentically, to outgrowing your network and seeking a new tribe. We hope you have found our stories inspiring and helpful for finding joy in your entrepreneurial journey.

If you are just beginning or looking to begin anew upon this journey, you can find joy in the process of becoming a kick-ass entrepreneur. First, work to become very content with where you are now, even as you strive to change and improve that situation.

Complacency and comparison are two of the greatest enemies of joy. Too many entrepreneurs are so focused on feeling dissatisfied with where they are that they never move forward. Find the joy in your current situation, and you will have no problem moving on to the next joyful place when you are ready to proceed.

We have talked about the importance of having strong reasons for doing what you are doing. But rather than focusing purely on success benchmarks, be more present and aware of each moment in the journey. When you slow down, pause to savor the amazing freedom of the entrepreneurial journey. Soon you will also wonder how you ever worked for someone else. You will feel inspired and empowered to move forward. Trust your journey. Finding your 'why' and experiencing the joy of doing something meaningful will help bring success.

Five Principles of Entrepreneurial Joy

Finding joy in this crazy journey every day is not always easy. I have found it helps to have a few principles or practices in place to help remind me how much joy is present in my life. The following are some of the principles I have put into place to find, recognize, receive and appreciate the joy in my journey.

1. Morning Rituals: You subconsciously carry the intentions with which you start your day for the next 16 hours. Imagine two different ways to start your day. In one scenario, you hit the snooze button for 45 minutes straight, jump into the shower, chug a cup of coffee and neglect to put any nourishing food into your body so you will not be late to work. In another scenario, you wake up at the crack of dawn to see the sunrise, relish a warm cup of coffee, meditate for twenty minutes, and consume a breakfast full of fruits and protein. Which do you think will result in a better day?

2. Acknowledgment: Give yourself a round of applause for having the awareness to demand more from your life.

Think about how many people spend their entire lives feeling unhappy until they are on their deathbeds. Instead of worrying so much about where you will be 3-5 years in the future, why not appreciate how far you have grown in the last 3-5 years. Did you ever imagine you would have done _____ (fill in the blank) by now? How awesome is it that you have?

3. Giving Back: In order to cultivate a much-needed sense of self-love, we can sometimes go to the extreme and become self-absorbed. I get it, and I have been there before. However, I feel more grounded and connected to the world when I am serving and inspiring others. We are all on separate journeys to happiness, and being able to help somebody else along their path is one of the greatest gifts you can give. Helping others to feel more joy will make your life much more joyful. I promise.

4. Social Connections: Remember your tribe?_The people with whom we associate can either be emotionally draining and force us to take on their problems, or they can elevate us to a higher level of fulfillment. The latter individuals are happy, healthy, and wealthy. So remember to associate with individuals that vibrate at this frequency because, before you know it, you will be on their level.

5. Travel: Want to know one of the coolest things about being a young entrepreneur who works virtually? I can take my business wherever I want! As long as I have Wi-Fi and my laptop, I am good to go. I can spontaneously decide to take a road trip to New York City without upsetting my work schedule. As you build your business, take some time to enjoy the fact that you can get up and go with much more freedom than when you had your old job.

Keep Moving Forward

Above all, find joy in the simple progress of moving forward. Walt Disney once said:

"Around here, we don't look backwards for very long. We keep moving forward, opening up new doors and doing new things, because we're curious…and curiosity keeps leading us down new paths."

As you move through your journey, consider these words. You might not progress in a straight line toward success. More likely, you will experience ebbs and flows, difficulties, and smooth sailings. There will be a lot that will test you as an entrepreneur, but keep moving forward and trust the journey. The most important thing to remember about your journey is that it is exactly that: *your* journey. So keep an open mind to new possibilities as they appear, embrace imperfections, and look for the joy that each day brings you.

Chapter 17:
The Journey Continues

In his book, *The Motivation Manifesto*, the #1 New York Times bestselling author & entrepreneur, Brendon Burchard, writes:

> "All great people of history...forged within themselves the courage to overcome their internal conflicts when it mattered most. In many ways, they are just like us: They worried. They procrastinated. They sometimes had lower opinions of their fellow human beings. But what made them celebrated, what pushed society forward, what gave birth to their legend, was their sheer will to overcome such impulses and to faithfully, actively, and lovingly fight for a better life for themselves and others. Let us learn from them, let us master ourselves, and let us now add our own chapter of courage to the good book of humanity."

The Journey Continues

It's been said many times before about life and business that the things that generally come easy aren't worth much at all. The same applies to our journey as entrepreneurs. The truth is: the road is hard, it's difficult and sometimes, you will want to give up. But that's what makes the journey that much more incredible – the fact that we are met with such great challenges and obstacles acting as a means of opportunity for us to become wiser, stronger and more educated. No one has ever said that this journey would be easy, but a lot of individuals have said it is more than worth it. And, we choose to agree.

As entrepreneurs, we forge the way to a better world for ourselves and for the rest of humanity. It is through us discovering what we love and having the courage to pursue passionate work that allows us to solve problems that will have a greater lasting impact on our world.

It is through the experiences that we go through now that will serve as great lessons for future entrepreneurs. It is in the courage we find today to do purposeful work that will impact our world tomorrow.

My friend, may you find the courage to not only be true to yourself, but also the courage to keep going even when that little voice in your head says 'stop, this is too difficult,' and to love the journey, remembering to always keep moving forward.

Section V

Bonus Chapters

Chapter 18:
Women in Entrepreneurship

While this section is targeted towards female entrepreneurs, the information here is of value to anyone who wants to make a positive change in the world.

As women, we are powerhouses that are wired to care for our friends, families, and communities. We pour ourselves into the things that set our souls on fire. This passion makes us natural entrepreneurs, particularly when building businesses that benefit humanity. The patience and dedication that enables us to nurture our loved ones is the same kind of tenacity needed to bring a successful business to life.

As a woman entrepreneur, I would like to share some pieces of advice that I have found helpful along the way.

1. You do not need to *only* market to women. I have found that many women entrepreneurs target women exclusively. I did that in the beginning, somewhat unwittingly, because I saw most other women entrepreneurs doing that. And yet, my first coaching client ended up being a man, and he was a great fit for me. If you have the notion that men will not take you seriously, scrap it. Unless you are making a product designed only for women, consider how you can help men as well. Changing the world means touching the lives of *all* types of people.

2. Be assertive. This is fairly obvious, but it should be restated. You will never make money if you do not charge what your products are worth. This does not mean ripping people off, but it does mean creating an equitable exchange of value. For instance if you sell coaching or information products, my recommendation is to give away a lot for free, but charge a premium for your paid material. Research different business models and find ones that will suit both your needs and those of your customers.

3. Build time for rest and regeneration into your schedule. It will make you more efficient. The standard (masculine) work model tells us to continually work harder, even if it means neglecting ourselves. But when you try to control yourself with brute force for an extended period of time, your brain ends up fighting you harder. Remember that you want a fulfilling life for yourself along with your business. It is really easy to get caught up in comparison, but this mentality drains you and can make you very unproductive. If you are looking for an excellent resource on staying balanced while you build your business, check out Arianna Huffington's book, *Thrive*.

4. Do not wait for your friends, family, or the rest of the world to believe in you. We have said this before, but as women, we are under even greater pressure to conform to other people's expectations. Therefore it is important to remember that the world might never believe in you, so you must have a reliable tribe for when you need support. There will also be times when you are completely on your own. This can be very scary. To get through it, you must learn to trust yourself completely and unapologetically.

5. Failure is not a reflection of you or your worth. It will happen, and you are not alone in it. Most women (and men as well) tend to internalize failure, but you can keep this in check. Approach each success and failure as a case study. Every time you think a destructive thought, ask yourself what you learned from the situation, and recognize that you are, in at least one way, richer from the experience.

6. Build your business in a way that feels right to you. You will not get the satisfaction you desire until your brand reflects your own mission, ideas, and values.

7. Acknowledge your successes. Reward yourself as you reach your milestones.

8. Enjoy the journey. Nothing is more exhilarating than experiencing your creations come to life with an open heart, experiencing the ups and downs fully and not closing yourself off.

The Two-Week Notice

As you gain momentum, you will develop your own rules and routines. You will gain confidence in every aspect of your work, and you will serve as a role model for others. You are going to do amazing things. The world needs you!

Chapter 19: Savings Accounts and Good Health

"Beware of little expenses. A small leak will sink a great ship." –Benjamin Franklin

Some days, the idea of being an entrepreneur may seem like a dream come true. And other times, you may wonder if you really have what it takes. Sometimes you will run into situations that will shake your confidence, but you will have no choice but to keep going. This bonus chapter is about dealing with a situation like that.

Most successful entrepreneurs will recommend that if you are starting out, you either:

1. Have a few projects lined up for yourself before exiting your job
2. Have money saved up to help pad your transition
3. Both, which will prove to be your best leverage

In my case, I had quite a bit of savings, which helped me travel the world and meet and connect with a lot more people. While I traveled, I had a few clients per month, so when my savings ran low I still had some income. Financially, I was doing well for myself.

Then I started feeling a strange knot in my neck.

Initially, I thought it was either due to an infection I got from a sickly friend or an injury from working out. I had no idea what it was, and I had other things on my mind, so I dismissed the knot for about two months. As time went by, and it did not go away, different thoughts started going through my head:

"I am not sick, I never get sick," and, "This better not be bad. I don't have international health insurance." And at other times, "I work out a lot. I've got to be healthy," or, "No, definitely can't be something wrong with me…but what if it is?"

The truth that I had been trying to avoid, more than anything, was that I was scared out of my mind. I was even scared to go to a doctor and get it looked at. "I have a long life ahead of me to live," I thought, "what if things don't come back in my favor?" Amidst all this noise, I finally mustered the courage to go have my first consultation.

The doctor felt the knot and requested that I go through a few stages of ultrasounds and biopsies to figure out what was going on. In my mind, I thought, "but I don't have in-

Savings Accounts and Good Health

surance, this is going to literally break me and take all the money I have." By this time, all the money I had saved up before I left my job was gone and the money I was making from client to client was sufficient, but I had not planned for a major event like this in my life.

From the results of my scans, the doctors could tell that the lymph nodes in my neck were strangely oversized, and gently told me that it could be a sign of leukemia but further tests would reveal the ultimate results.

That day, I left the doctor's office tired, confused and scared. In the past, I have seen many, many people lose their battle to leukemia and cancer, and I was afraid to lose the battle as well. On top of that, growing up with the dream to work in Hollywood, I had often seen very dramatic pictures painted about health and illness.

I broke down when I spoke to my mother, herself a cancer survivor, as she reassured me that everything would be okay. I would have to wait almost a week before the doctor's office had an opening for me to get a full range of biopsies. That week was even tougher because I was abroad. My normal support group was thousands of miles away. I was alone and I was terrified.

The day after the biopsies, the doctor asked me to come into the office to review my results. "Alex, we have done 12 tests in total for you and I am happy to say that you will be okay. Your lymph nodes are still enlarged, but it is not directly linked to any illnesses."

"So I'm okay?"

"Yes, you are okay," he said as I shook his hand with a tear in my eye.

This is the kind of situation I mentioned at the beginning of this chapter. Many times we think, "Oh, it won't happen to me." I thought the same thing until it did. In fact, at that time, I found myself at a crossroads, having to decide between risking my health and spending money I did not have.

Luckily, I realized which was more important to me before it was too late.

I wanted to share this as a bonus chapter not only to point out the importance of having a "rainy day" emergency fund, but also to tie up the importance of our other chapters on good health. I let my ego get in the way for months because I thought I was too fit, in shape or healthy to have anything wrong with me.

Even when we think that nothing can happen to us, it is still critical to practice preventative self-care. This means taking care of both our health and our bank accounts — especially in building up that emergency fund I mentioned. Doing these things will not prevent every difficult experience from happening, but it will help us get through them and move forward.

The rainy day may come for us all. Have your umbrella ready.

Chapter 20: Creating a For-Benefit Organization

Have you ever been at a place in your life where you knew you had to do something fundamentally different?

For me, this happened twice during the first year of my organization's operation. I can say with confidence that if I had not changed direction then, that my business would have stalled or worse, gone under.

I started No Typical Moments with immense altruistic intentions. Within 90 days of starting, the pressure of generating a revenue stream obliterated those intentions. Unless I wanted to declare bankruptcy by the age of 24, I needed to at least break even with my expenses. But because of this added tension, I lost my sense of purpose. I no longer felt like the company had a reason for existing aside from generating cash to pay my bills. I was torn. I needed the business to work so I could fund my own survival, but I could not talk enthusiastically about the company because I did not believe it was making the world a better place.

I decided to ditch the profit at all cost mentality and adopted a one-for-one model like *a verynice design studio* has pioneered. With every paying client, we would allocate pro-bono services to an underserved non-profit organization. I believed that in the service of others, I would create a new purposeful and fulfilling direction for the organization.

As luck would have it, adopting a for-benefit model actually worked! By giving away our services for free, No Typical Moments began to land more paying clients. By February, I had replaced the monthly income I had lost at the job I quit.

We were working with amazing non-profits from around the world such as Team Tassy, Haitian Families First and the Meltwater Entrepreneurial School of Technology. We even helped Haitian Families First raise over $13,000 on a crowdfunding campaign. I was on cloud nine.

I soon started to realize, however, that things were not quite where I wanted them to be yet. Our clientele was divided into two groups. The first group consisted of amazing non-profits that were making a making positive impact and changing people's lives. The other group was a collection of paying clients who were not doing anything *un*ethical, but who were not really helping or serving the world, either. Their missions were not aligned with our own.

Creating a For-Benefit Organization

So I put myself in the position of a marketing representative that works at a purpose-driven company. Just like a consumer who is more likely to buy from a brand that she knows is ethical, would a for-benefit organization not want to hire another for-benefit company to help with their marketing strategy?

After talking with a handful of individuals and potential clients, I discovered the answer was a resounding yes. These people wanted to align with organizations with similar missions and values so they could build a tribe of advocates.

I decided to take another bold stand and rebrand No Typical Moments across the board. From then on, we would only work with businesses whose missions focused on making the world a better place. We also decided to align with the GameChangers 500 instead of the Fortune 500. The GameChangers 500 is a network of the world's top 500 for-benefit organizations. Organizations that grace the list include Zappos, Whole Foods and Facebook, to name a few. Rather than pitching to work with the richest companies, NTM would now align with the companies working to do the most good in the world.

There are continuously questions that arise as to how to create a mission first organization that is for-profit, there are fantastic frameworks being built. For example, GameChangers 500 ranks these organizations around nine badges of success aside from revenue.

They include:

Why You Are in Business: To Maximize Benefit, Not Just Profit

Meet the Mission: Clearly defining your mission, using a theory of change to help determine your direction, and developing metrics to measure your progress.

What Your Business Offers: Products or Services That Create a Better World

Depth of Impact: Your product or service helps people and/or the planet thrive, often through the introduction of a new innovation.

Scale of Impact: Your product or service is designed to scale to larger regions, often through industry collaboration, partnerships, open-sourcing, franchising or other models of dissemination that help you expand your positive impact.

How You Run Your Business: Positively Impacts People and the Planet

Exceptional Work Environment: Environments that are fun, inspiring and an evolutionary leap beyond the beige cubicle.

Empowered Employees: Autonomy, servant leadership, generous benefits, constant learning, and hiring based on strengths, shared values and passion for the mission.
Everyone Wins: Care and concern for customers, supplies, distributors, investors and the community.

Creating a For-Benefit Organization

Earth Friendly Office: Choosing eco-friendly supplies and suppliers and minimizing waste, water, and carbon-based energy.

Eco Design: Designing your products, services and manufacturing processes to be carbon-neutral, zero waste, and non-toxic.

Replenish the Planet: Using your business as a platform to spread environmental awareness and to support environmental causes.

Resources like those above will allow you to emulate the kinds of organizations that you aspire to create.

Works Cited

Berman, Gillian. Twenty-Somethings' Debt Burden Averages $45,000, Report Finds. 21 March 2012. 1 March 2015 <http://www.huffingtonpost.com/2012/03/21/twenty-somethings-debt_n_1368128.html>.

Burchard, Brendon (2014). *The Motivation Manifesto: 9 Declarations to Claim Your Personal Power*. Carlsbad, CA. Hay House.

Carroll, Jim. gen-y & gen connect. 21 January 2015. 1 March 2015 <https://www.jimcarroll.com/category/blog/gen-y-gen-connect/#.VVpBQdrBzRa>.

Dinsmore, Scott. Live Off Your Passion. 2014. 1 March 2015 <http://loypcourse.wpengine.com/>.
Fairchild, Caroline. Women CEOs in the Fortune 1000: By the numbers. 8 July 2014. 1 March 2015 <http://fortune.com/2014/07/08/women-ceos-fortune-500-1000/>.

Fry, Rakesh Kochhar and Richard. Wealth inequality has widened along racial, ethnic lines since end of Great Recession. 14 December 2014. 1 March 2015 <http://www.pewresearch.org/fact-tank/2014/12/12/racial-wealth-gaps-great-recession/>.

Graves, Jada A. How to Negotiate Salary Like a Man. 29 May 2014. 1 March 2015

<http://money.usnews.com/money/careers/articles/2014/05/29/how-to-negotiate-salary-like-a-man>.

Louis, Meera. $1 Trillion Debt Crushes Business Dreams of U.S. Students. 3 June 2013. 1 March 2015 <http://www.bloomberg.com/news/articles/2013-06-06/-1-trillion-debt-crushes-business-dreams-of-u-s-students>.

McGregor, Jena. Only 13 percent of people worldwide actually like going to work. 10 October 2013. 1 March 2015 <http://www.washingtonpost.com/blogs/on-leadership/wp/2013/10/10/only-13-percent-of-people-worldwide-actually-like-going-to-work/>.

Nelson, Trevor. Philanthropy and Millennials: Get On Board Or Get Left Behind. 6 June 2013. 1 March 2015 <http://www.huffingtonpost.com/trevor-neilson/philanthrop-and-millennia_b_3269238.html>.

Pew Research. Motivating a Young Workforce. 11 January 2011. 1 March 2015 <http://tribehr.com/blog/motivating-a-young-workforce-infographic/>.

Picci, Aimee. Millennials face savings time bomb. 10 November 2014. 1 March 2015 <http://www.cbsnews.com/news/the-millennial-generations-savings-time-bomb/>.
PwC. Engaging and Empowering Millennials. New York, NY, 2014.

Rasmussen College. "Economic Envy: Millennial Entrepreneurship Ascending." 21 October 2013. 1 March 2015 <http://www.youtern.com/thesavvyintern/index.php/2013/10/21/gen-y-believes-in-being-their-own-boss-infographic/>.

Schawbel, Dan. <u>74 Of The Most Interesting Facts About The Millennial Generation - See more at: http://danschawbel.com/blog/74-of-the-most-interesting-facts-about-the-millennial-generation/#sthash.sntVL5wy.dpuf</u>. 25 June 2013. 1 March 2015 <http://danschawbel.com/blog/74-of-the-most-interesting-facts-about-the-millennial-generation/>.

Sen, Ashish Kumar. <u>Bookmark: The Prof Who Keeps His Shirt On</u>. 28 June 2010. 1 March 2015 <http://www.outlookindia.com/article/bookmark-the-prof-who-keeps-his-shirt-on-/265875>.

Shontell, Alyson. <u>15 Seriously Disturbing Facts About Your Job</u>. 11 February 2011. 1 March 2015 <http://www.businessinsider.com/disturbing-facts-about-your-job-2011-2#the-average-person-spends-90000-hours-at-work-over-their-lifetime-2>.

Temple, James. <u>Salman Khan, math master of the Internet</u>. 14 December 2009. 1 March 2015 <http://www.sfgate.com/business/article/Salman-Khan-math-master-of-the-Internet-3278578.php>.

World Bank. <u>GDP (current US$)</u>. 2015. 1 March 2015 <http://data.worldbank.org/indicator/NY.GDP.MKTP.CD>.

About the Authors

Alex Echols is a best-selling author, the co-creator of the business-consulting course, *The Blueprint*, and an investor in companies in lifestyle, education and travel. He is most of all, proud to be a cancer survivor. He can be followed at www.alexechols.com

Andrew Gottlieb is the founder and CEO of No Typical Moments. His organization's mission is to empower 50 million lives by 2020 by offering digital marketing solutions to for-benefit organizations. His journey can be followed at www.notypicalmoments.com

Sulinya Ramanan is a multi-passionate entrepreneur. She has founded a lifestyle and wellness brand in her name and is working to improve the food system, from agricultural safety and ethics to sustainability and making healthful options affordable and accessible to everyone. She can be found at www.sulinya.com

Thank you for accompanying us on this journey :)

If you've enjoyed reading this book, please leave us a great review on our Amazon page.

www.ingramcontent.com/pod-product-compliance
Lightning Source LLC
Chambersburg PA
CBHW031629210526
45464CB00004B/1810